ADVENT WITH
OUR LADY OF FATIMA

Donna-Marie Cooper O'Boyle

Advent with
OUR LADY
of FATIMA

SOPHIA INSTITUTE PRESS
Manchester, New Hampshire

Sophia Institute Press
Box 5284, Manchester, NH 03108
1-800-888-9344

www.SophiaInstitute.com

Sophia Institute Press® is a registered trademark of Sophia Institute.

Library of Congress Cataloging-in-Publication Data

Names: O'Boyle, Donna-Marie Cooper, author.
Title: Advent with Our Lady of Fatima / Donna-Marie Cooper O'Boyle.
Description: Manchester, New Hampshire : Sophia Institute Press, 2018. |
    Includes bibliographical references.
Identifiers: LCCN 2018039598 | ISBN 9781622826506 (hardcover : alk. paper)
Subjects: LCSH: Advent—Prayers and devotions. | Mary, Blessed Virgin,
    Saint—Devotion to. | Fatima, Our Lady of. | Catholic Church—Prayers and devotions.
Classification: LCC BX2170.A4 O26 2018 | DDC 242/.332—dc23 LC record available at https://lccn.loc.gov/2018039598

First printing

With love for my children:
Justin, Chaldea, Jessica,
Joseph, and Mary-Catherine,
and my grandchildren:
Shepherd and Leo

CONTENTS

Week 3: Joy
THE JUBILANT JOY OF THE FATIMA
MESSAGE WITH ST. JOHN PAUL II

Week 4: Love
OUR LADY OF FATIMA AND MOTHER TERESA
TEACH US AUTHENTIC, ABIDING LOVE

INTRODUCTION

Advent begins on the Sunday closest to the feast of St. Andrew the Apostle, November 30. This special season includes four Sundays and four weeks of preparation. At times, the last week of Advent is shortened because of the timing of Christmas.

Our Lady of Fatima is very naturally related to the Advent season. First, because she is the Mother of God, which means she has much to do with the Nativity of the Lord! She carried Jesus in her womb for nine months and gave birth to Him! As well, at Fatima, Mary came down from heaven to give the world a warn-ing—to wake us from our slumber. She loves her children and does not want any one of them to perish. Advent calls us to wake up and keep watch—to "keep awake" (1 Thess. 5:6).

Stick close by to Our Lady of Fatima as you embrace the season of Advent—a period of expectant joy as you spiritually prepare your heart and soul through this unique devotional. Each day dur-ing Advent, journey with Our Lady and with reflections on hope, love, joy, and peace.

The theme of Advent is one of longing—of yearning for Christ. Yet we are also cautioned, "Watch therefore, for you do not know on what day your Lord is coming.... Therefore you also must be ready; for the Son of man is coming at an hour you do not expect" (Matt. 24:42, 44). *Advent with Our Lady of Fatima* will help you to stay the course and not get caught up with the holiday shopping frenzy, which can distract us from Christ during this holy season. Instead, do your best to embrace the twofold meaning of Advent—the expectant waiting and preparation for the celebration of the Nativity of Jesus as well as the ardent desire for His Second Coming. Through Church teachings and compelling stories of saintly friends, page by page, you will learn and refresh your faith as you reflect and meditate upon the reality of Christ at the center of your life.[1]

Pilgrimage day by day through Advent with Our Lady of Fatima at your side. It can be a life-transforming pilgrimage for you. It certainly was an exceptional spiritual journey for me as I wrote this book. May God bless your journey! Stay awake!

---

[1] I have endeavored to provide complete information about the sources of all the quotes contained herein, but sometimes that has not been possible.

Week 1: Hope

OUR LADY OF FATIMA AND FR. ANDREW APOSTOLI, CFR, BRING HOPE TO OUR HEARTS

Your lives must be like mine: quiet and hidden, in un-
ceasing union with God, pleading for humanity and
preparing the world for the second coming of God.

—Our Blessed Mother to St. Faustina (*Diary* 625)

On this First Sunday of Advent, we light our first Advent-wreath candle. It represents hope! Strive to live your Faith fully alive with hope during this week of Advent. This week we will look at Advent with Our Lady of Fatima at our side and through the eyes and heart of Fr. Andrew Apostoli, CFR. Fr. Andrew was a beloved friar of the Franciscan Friars of the Renewal and a world-leading Fatima expert.

FR. ANDREW EXEMPLIFIES GREAT HOPE THROUGH PERSEVERING PRAYER

Our Lady, the only one who can say this, said that when enough people do as I say, my triumph will come, and that will bring peace into the world. If we don't do what she says, I don't see where there is great hope.

—Fr. Andrew Apostoli, personal interview with the author

Read

Fr. Andrew was a tireless worker in Our Lord's vineyard—a beautiful, loving, humble soul. I am blessed to call him my friend, and I have loved working with him on several EWTN television shows.

Fr. Andrew was ordained to the priesthood by Venerable Archbishop Fulton Sheen on March 16, 1967. In 1987, he co-founded the Franciscan Friars of the Renewal with Fr. Benedict Groeschel and six other Capuchin friars, and later he founded the Franciscan Sisters of the Renewal. Fr. Andrew loved the Blessed Mother very much and preached extensively on Our Lady of Fatima, becoming a reliable and trusted Fatima expert. Dear Fr. Andrew went home to his eternal reward on the feast of St. Lucy, December 13, 2017.

This humble Friar was serious about his prayer life and stayed true to his commitments and responsibilities to prayer. His daily Holy Hour and Rosary gave power to his work and his apostolate. The floor boards in the back of the chapel at the friary where he lived are worn down by his continual walking back and forth while praying his many Rosaries. The friars have told me that he would do this during his Holy Hours because he wanted to make sure he stayed awake! As well, he didn't want to disappoint Mother Mary.

WEEK 1: HOPE

In the passage that begins today's Advent reflection, Fr. Andrew mentions that Mary asked the faithful to do certain things and then her Immaculate Heart would triumph. Those requests were to convert our hearts and sin no more, to pray a daily Rosary for peace, and to make sacrifices for sinners because, as she told the children she appeared to at Fatima, many souls go to hell because no one prays for them. As well, she asked for the conversion of Russia and for the Five First Saturdays Devotions.

Fr. Andrew was a very hopeful soul. Yet we notice that he said, "I don't see where there is great hope" if we don't do what the Blessed Mother has asked. That's because he was aware of the state of our sinful world today. He and countless others believe that Our Lady of Fatima offered the world a beautiful and hopeful plan for peace. Yes, it does require effort on our part to pray the Rosary, to do the Five First Saturdays Devotions, and to offer sacrifices and do penance. It is for the good of our souls, as well as to help convert sinners, and to bring peace to the world. In addition, although Fr. Andrew knew well that the faithful were not yet fulfilling their responsibilities to prayer according to Our Lady's requests, he possessed great hope in the Blessed Mother's promises. He didn't give up — all the way until his last breath. He kept on preaching about Fatima. He continued his many Rosaries. He wore out the floor boards at the back of the chapel!

Reflect

Take time to reflect on your prayer life. Are you "wearing out the floor boards" in your spiritual life? Can you try to step up your prayers this Advent? Try to find ways to prepare your heart for the upcoming Nativity of Our Lord Jesus, as well as for His Second Coming. What steps can you take today to look for silence in which to pray? Can you spend less time on media and television, so you can give your heart fully to God in prayer? Ponder a sacrifice you can make to offer in reparation for sinners.

Pray

Dear Jesus and Our Lady of Fatima, please help me to slow down and to be more attentive to the whispers of the Holy Spirit this Advent. Our Lady of Fatima, please pray for me.

*Pray the Rosary today in honor of Our Lady
of Fatima and for peace in the world.*

Act

Offer a sacrifice in reparation for sinners, as Our Lady of Fatima has asked. Strive to convert your heart today with God's grace and Mother Mary's help, remembering that conversion of heart should be a daily occurrence.

FR. ANDREW EMPHASIZES THE GREAT IMPORTANCE OF CONVICTIONS

It was as a child that I myself first heard about the message of Our Lady of Fatima. I saw one of the first movies about the Fatima events, and it left an impression on me all through my years of growing up. I never forgot it.

—Fr. Andrew Apostoli to the author

Read

The Fatima message and events left a lasting impression on Fr. Andrew that he couldn't ignore. The Queen of Heaven's powerful holy message and the family Rosary he prayed as a child were the dynamic embers that, together with the breath of the Holy Spirit, mightily stoked flames of desire for the priesthood in the young man's heart.

Early on in religious life, his novice master said something that also captured Fr. Andrew's attention. "When I was a young novice over fifty years ago," the novice master recalled, "my novice master repeatedly said: 'Form your convictions now, because you will have to live the rest of your life based on them.' That was good advice." Fr. Andrew indeed took this to his heart and applied it to his daily life. He said, "One of the things we must be absolutely convinced of is that our Lady is calling each one of us to be involved in this struggle." Fr. Andrew was referring to the spiritual battle for souls that is waged all around us and that certainly involves each one of us. If it doesn't involve us, then there is a problem, because every faithful soul is immersed in spiritual battle all the way to his eternal reward. This battle, for the most part, is invisible, so we might not take notice. But for spiritual survival, we must. Fr. Andrew encourages us, "Convictions produce doers." He added, "Someone once said: 'One person with a belief is equal in force to ninety-nine people who merely have an interest.'" Fr. Andrew asks, "Do we really believe in what our Lady is asking of us? Are we convinced of its importance, or are we merely interested in it?"[2] These are important words for us to ponder in our hearts.

Fr. Andrew doesn't want us to be wishy-washy in our Faith. We need to be convinced of its truth. Our Lady of Fatima gave us a peace plan from heaven and insists that the Rosary can stop wars, prevent catastrophes, and bring about world peace. Fr. Andrew said, "There's no other plan from heaven that is so specific, for what we're going through now. The Blessed Mother spelled it out. Prayer, penance, the Five First Saturdays Devotions — and live a good, holy life. That's the answer."[3] We need to immerse ourselves more firmly in Our Lady of Fatima's messages and become "doers" in living out her requests and in promoting the messages. This will inevitably benefit our own souls and the souls of others.

Reflect

Will you be a person with conviction, anchored in hope? God calls you to be a "doer." That doesn't mean that you need to run a marathon, build a cathedral, or undertake some other huge endeavor. A doer can do a lot even while sitting still or kneeling! A lot can be accomplished through your servant prayers. Think about it. While you're ruminating, be sure to think of ways to prepare your heart for the Nativity of Our Lord Jesus, as well as for His Second Coming. Try to find a bit of silence in which to pray. Try hard to carve

[2] Andrew Apostoli, *Fatima for Today: The Urgent Marian Message of Hope* (San Francisco: Ignatius Press, 2010), chap. 18.

[3] To the author in a personal interview and in Donna-Marie Cooper O'Boyle, *Our Lady of Fatima: One Hundred Years of Stories, Prayers, and Devotions* (Cincinnati: Servant, 2017), 11–12.

out a solid time for prayer and meditation each day during this holy season. Finally, pray about a sacrifice you can make to offer in reparation for sinners, and carry it out. Do it!

Pray

Dear Jesus and Our Lady of Fatima, please help me to be more cognizant this Advent season about the battle for souls. Help me to be more proactive and convicted in my Faith. Our Lady of Fatima, please pray for me.

*Pray the Rosary today in honor of Our Lady
of Fatima and for peace in the world.*

Act

What sacrifice can you make in reparation for sinners, as Our Lady of Fatima has asked? Can you strive to convert your heart today with God's grace and Mother Mary's help, remembering that conversion of heart should be a daily occurrence? Be sure to put your convictions into action!

A MIRACLE OF HOPE IS DISCOVERED IN FATIMA

If we live the message that Our Lady gave us at Fatima, our personal faith will grow much stronger. At the same time, it will have an increased effect on the very life and mission of the Church, which is the mystical Body of Christ.

—Fr. Andrew Apostoli, *Soul Magazine*, Fall 2012

Read

We can be assured that Fr. Andrew instructed his Friars well through many teachings and spiritual exercises, but also through his example of prayer and perseverance and his filial devotion to Our Lady of Fatima. In the hundredth-anniversary year of the apparitions of Our Lady of Fatima, Fr. Andrew was scheduled to be the spiritual director on a pilgrimage I was leading to Fatima, Portugal. As the pilgrimage drew near, Fr. Andrew told me that his superiors informed him that he could not go; it would be much too strenuous for him. His health had begun to deteriorate in the few months prior. It was one health issue after another, and Fr. Andrew courageously fought for a restoration of his health, but also accepted God's holy will throughout the suffering, wholeheartedly offering it up to God for the conversion of sinners, as Our Lady of Fatima had requested. Redemptive suffering was something Fr. Andrew had taken seriously and had preached passionately. Now he was intensely living it, too.

As much as I knew I would miss having Fr. Andrew by my side on the pilgrimage, I was deeply concerned for his health and well-being, and I totally accepted the change of plan and would continue to pray for my dear friend. Another Franciscan Friar of the Renewal, Fr. Luke Fletcher, was appointed as the spiritual

director for the pilgrimage. Fr. Andrew highly recommended
him to me, and with a smile, he added that Fr. Luke had a "very
long beard!" The friars have jokingly expressed that the length
of their beards denotes the level of their wisdom! But, all joking
aside, it was a blessing to have Fr. Luke on my pilgrimage. I'd
like to share a compelling story that he shared with me later.

Fr. Luke was ordained on May 17, 2003. For an ordination
gift, his cousins gave him a vestment set with a custom-made
stole with special embroidery that included his name. Fr. Luke
enjoyed the vestments very much, but about eleven years later,
his stole went missing. He told me, "I had been looking high and
low. I asked all the friars, but no one knew a thing." Three years
passed and still no sign of the stole.

In November 2017, Fr. Luke was surprised to be invited
on another pilgrimage to Fatima in Fr. Andrew's place (this
was after the pilgrimage he went on with me). It was a beautiful pilgrimage, during which Fr. Luke had heartily prayed for a
renewal of his priestly vows. Something quite extraordinary and
totally unexpected happened the day he was to head back to the
United States. We can even call it miraculous! Fr. Luke was able
to wear his long-lost stole at the last Mass he would celebrate in
Fatima on that pilgrimage.

Allow me to explain through Fr. Luke. "When we opened
the sacristy at 4 a.m., the stole was sitting out on the counter." Fr. Luke had the key to the sacristy and had been spiritual
leader to the only group using the sacristy that entire week. He
continued, "It is custom-made, one of a kind, so I immediately
realized that it was my missing stole. I asked the other friars, and
no one had brought it." We can imagine Fr. Luke's excitement
over finding his long-lost stole and in such an unexpected, yet
amazingly significant place. How in the world did it get there?
Immediate questions might have been swirling around in this

friar's brain, but he really had no doubts. He shared, "Finding that missing stole in that sacristy was a real sign, a signal grace that my prayer for renewal in my vocation was being answered in a dramatic way." He said, "There is no explanation for how that stole went missing and showed up in that sacristy in Fatima over three years later." He added, "It was not there all week. On our last day, there it was, waiting for me, set out on the counter." On top of that, Fr. Luke exclaimed, "All in the land of St. Anthony!" We might say that Fr. Luke received a beautiful Fatima miracle from the Blessed Mother, distributor of amazing graces. Perhaps, St. Anthony, patron saint of lost objects might have had his hand in it, too.

Reflect

Our Lord and Our Lady know exactly what we need and when we need it. Finding his stole, such a significant and meaningful part of his priestly vestments, was an absolute positive sign to Fr. Luke that his prayers had been answered. Answered prayers fill our hearts with great hope. Take time to reflect on your life and prayers of hope. As well, prepare your heart for the upcoming Nativity of Our Lord Jesus and for His Second Coming. Ponder an earnest sacrifice you can make to offer in reparation for sinners.

Pray

Dear Jesus and Our Lady of Fatima, please help me to pray more and even to expect miracles this Advent. Our Lady of Fatima, please pray for me.

*Pray the Rosary today in honor of Our Lady
of Fatima and for peace in the world.*

WEEK 1: HOPE

Act

Offer a sacrifice in reparation for sinners, as Our Lady of Fatima has asked. Strive to convert your heart today with God's grace and Mother Mary's help, remembering that conversion of heart should be a daily occurrence.

OUR LADY URGES
HOPE FOR HEAVEN

What Our Lady spoke of to the three little children of Fatima was a message that emphasizes that heaven is real. It also makes it clear that our supreme responsibility is to live in such a way that we may be found worthy to enter the kingdom of heaven.

—Fr. Andrew Apostoli, *Soul Magazine*, Fall 2012

Read

Lived well, the season of Advent can help us meditate upon our eternal life as well as the need to help others get to heaven. Our Lady emphasizes that heaven is real and that we need to live holy lives to get there one day, but it's important to recognize that hell is very real, too, and is a sure consequence for unrepented sin. Fr. Andrew said, "Mary also warned us that the alternative [to leading a holy life] would be to lose our souls in hell forever! Mary's message, then, clearly sets before us a choice of life or death, of eternal bliss or eternal misery." He added, "She was deeply concerned that all her children would be saved, and none would be lost. She expressed this again with great sorrow." Fr. Andrew pointed out that "she told the children in her August apparition: 'Pray, pray very much and make sacrifices for sinners; for many souls go to hell, because there are none to sacrifice themselves and to pray for them.'"[4]

We know that Our Lady of Fatima also showed the children a vivid vision of hell in her July apparition. For one frightening moment the three innocent shepherd children saw the darkness, heard the shrieking demons, and witnessed the souls of the

[4] Ibid.

27

damned burning in hell. Lucia would later say that if the Blessed Mother hadn't assured them earlier that they would be going to heaven, they surely would have died of fright. Yet, as horrifying as it was for them to see the reality of hell, the children became passionate about praying for the souls of sinners and in promoting Our Lady's messages. During that July apparition, Mary told the children that God was establishing devotion to her Immaculate Heart. She gave us great hope when she said, "In the end, my Immaculate Heart will triumph ... and a period of peace will be granted to the world."[5]

As mentioned earlier, Fr. Andrew was ordained by Venerable Fulton Sheen, who was a renowned theologian and a beloved communicator known for his preaching on radio and television and who is considered a saint of the twentieth century. He was a great promoter of the Rosary and Our Lady of Fatima's messages. Father Andrew became the vice-postulator of Archbishop Fulton Sheen's cause of canonization and very connected to his work, stating, "I felt we cannot let his voice grow silent in the Catholic Church. He still has so much to offer."[6] Archbishop Sheen was much more than a mentor to Fr. Andrew, who said, "St. Francis is my seraphic father in my religious vocation, and Bishop Sheen is my father in Christ for my priestly vocation."[7]

Now that I've explained the connection between these two holy souls, I'll share a story about Archbishop Sheen and the power of sacrificial love and perseverance to aid a sinner at death's door.

A woman pleaded with Archbishop Sheen to help her dying brother. She was extremely concerned for his eternal fate

[5] Ibid., 57.
[6] Joseph Pronechen, "Father Apostoli on Archbishop Sheen," *National Catholic Register*, March 7, 2014.
[7] Ibid.

and explained that he was not just a sinner but was unrepentant for very evil things he had done in his life. Archbishop Sheen agreed to visit him in the hospital. The woman told him that her brother had already thrown seventeen priests out of his room. So, the archbishop decided to make his every visit extremely short—about fifteen seconds. The man asked him to leave. The archbishop persisted in his mission and ended up visiting the man for forty nights! Each visit was extremely short. Toward the end, he brought the Blessed Sacrament and entered the man's room. After a while, the man told him to leave, and the archbishop explained that he had someone with him. He told him it was Jesus, and the man quieted down for a bit. Then, once again, the man told him to leave his room. Before leaving, the archbishop bent close to the man's cancerous face and begged him to ask God for His mercy before it was too late, because he would die that night. The man said he knew he was going to die and straightaway ordered Archbishop Sheen out of his room.

On the way out, Archbishop Sheen stopped by the nurse's station and asked her to call him at any time if the man needed him and he would rush back. His phone rang at 3:00 a.m. It was the nurse. She informed the archbishop that the man had just died. We can imagine Archbishop Sheen's heart sinking, learning of this death and not having been able to be at the man's side to offer confession or an anointing. The nurse then explained that as soon as Archbishop Sheen left, the man cried out loudly for Jesus' mercy—over and over again for hours until he died! Archbishop Sheen never gave up on that sinner. His sacrificial love and perseverance helped a hardened sinner to turn away from hell and toward heaven.

The Fatima message is very much about converting our hearts and leading holy lives, as well as praying and offering sacrifices for sinners and praying the Rosary daily for peace in the world. Certainly, we want to live eternally happy in heaven one day. But we must also have a generous attitude in making reparation on behalf of sinners who might not have anyone to pray for them. Our Lady of Fatima calls us to stay close to her Son Jesus and to have a devotion to her Immaculate Heart.

Reflect

How will you help a sinner? Can you teach the truth about hell and the consequences of sin? Can you lovingly suggest Confession to someone in need of it? Take time to prepare your heart for the upcoming Nativity of Our Lord Jesus, as well as for His Second Coming. Try hard to carve out solid times for prayer and meditation each day. Take time to sit still with God—and listen. Ponder sacrifices you can make in reparation for sinners, and be sure to carry them out.

Pray

Dear Jesus and Our Lady of Fatima, please help me to aid sinners with my prayers, sacrifices, and actions this Advent. Our Lady of Fatima, please pray for me.

Pray the Rosary today in honor of Our Lady of Fatima and for peace in the world.

Act

Offer a sacrifice in reparation for sinners, as Our Lady of Fatima has asked. Through prayer, strive to convert your heart today with God's grace and Mother Mary's help, remembering that conversion of heart should be a daily occurrence.

THURSDAY

OUR LADY'S SPIRITUAL FORMATION PROGRAM

This devotion is one of the most important requests Our Lady made, yet probably the most neglected. I call it "Our Lady's spiritual formation program." She requested it along with the consecration of Russia for its conversion. The Pope has done his part, but are we carrying out this devotion in sufficient numbers to bring about the conversion of sinners that Our Lady said are needed for peace in the world?

—Fr. Andrew Apostoli, *National Catholic Register* interview, April 29, 2011

Read

As a Dorothean nun, on December 10, 1925, Sr. Lucia was visited by the Blessed Mother, who came along with the Christ Child. Mary showed Sr. Lucia her Immaculate Heart, encircled with thorns. She asked her for compassion and told her about the Five First Saturdays Devotions, otherwise known as the Communion of Reparation. Sr. Lucia's spiritual director asked her to write down the details of that visit and to put them in the third person. This is what Sr. Lucia wrote:

> On December 10, 1925, the most holy Virgin appeared to her, and by her side, elevated on a luminous cloud, was [the Christ] child. The most holy Virgin rested her hand on [Sr. Lucia's] shoulder, and as she did so, she showed her a heart encircled in thorns, which she was holding in her other hand. At the same time, the [Christ] Child said: "Have compassion on the Heart of your most holy Mother, covered with thorns, with which ungrateful men pierce it at every moment, and there is no one to make an act of reparation to remove them." Then the most holy Virgin said: "Look, my daughter, at my Heart, surrounded with thorns with which ungrateful men pierce me at every moment by their blasphemies and ingratitude. You

at least try to console me and say that I promise to assist at the hour of death, with the graces necessary for salvation, all those who, on the first Saturday of five consecutive months, shall confess [their sins], receive Holy Communion, recite five decades of the Rosary, and keep me company for fifteen minutes while meditating on the fifteen mysteries of the Rosary, with the intention of making reparation to me."[8]

The Blessed Mother laid out a beautiful plan of reparation to be done on the first Saturday of five consecutive months with the intention of making reparation for the sins of ingratitude and blasphemy committed against her:

† Go to confession on the first Saturday or during the week before or after.
† Receive Holy Communion (not necessarily during a Mass, though that is beneficial).
† Pray five decades of the Rosary.
† Keep the Blessed Mother company for fifteen minutes while meditating on the mysteries of the Rosary.

Father Andrew explained that the Five First Saturdays Devotions are one of the most important requests of Our Lady and he questioned whether we are carrying this out in sufficient numbers to bring about the Blessed Mother's triumph. I have heard him say many times that he believes that this is the most neglected part of Our Lady of Fatima's requests. This reminds me of going to confession to Fr. Andrew when I first met him. He told me then that it is good to get into the habit of going to confession monthly — if possible, on the first Saturday of the

---

[8] *Fatima, in Lucia's Own Words: Sister Lucia's Memoirs*, ed. Louis Kondor, S.V.D., trans. Dominican Nuns of the Perpetual Rosary (n.p.: Fatima Postulation Center, 1976), 195.

month. In this way, we can participate in the Five First Saturdays Devotions.

The Blessed Mother assured Sr. Lucia that she will "assist at the hour of death, with the graces necessary for salvation" those who make the Five First Saturdays Devotions. What a great promise! We should all be eager to step up to the plate! Fr. Andrew pointed out that we shouldn't be concerned only with our own souls but also with the souls who need help. Specifically, he said, "to make five first Saturdays for ourselves to obtain the promise and then stop would be to neglect our responsibility in genuine Christian love for the salvation of the souls of our neighbors, which would be inconsistent with the second greatest commandment." He went on to explain, "Our motivation in the practice of this devotion should not be merely the promise associated with it. Rather, we should practice it all of our lives for the sake of the souls of our neighbors as well as our own." He added that many souls are lost due to the lack of generous souls: "Our Lady told us that souls are being lost to hell because there is no one to make reparation for their sins. She implored us on their behalf. How can we deny her?"[9]

Reflect

Let's not deny our dear Blessed Mother, who lovingly requests our prayers and sacrifices to save souls. Do your best to commit to the Five First Saturdays Devotions. Remember the upcoming Nativity of Our Lord Jesus, which may seem far off right now, but it is surely approaching. Prepare your heart to welcome Him at Christmas as well as at His Second Coming. Though at times it may seem impossible to find, search for a bit of silence in

---

[9] World Apostolate of Fatima, *The First Saturday Devotion* (Washington, NJ: World Apostolate of Fatima, n.d.).

which to pray. Ponder a sacrifice you can make to offer in reparation for sinners.

Pray

Dear Jesus and Our Lady of Fatima, please help me to be much more generous with my prayers and sacrifices this Advent. Our Lady of Fatima, please pray for me.

Pray the Rosary today in honor of Our Lady of Fatima and for peace in the world.

Act

Offer a sacrifice in reparation for sinners, as Our Lady of Fatima has asked. Pray for the graces to convert your heart today with Mother Mary's help, remembering that conversion of heart should be a daily occurrence.

HOPE FOR THE WORLD IS WRAPPED IN SACRIFICE AND PRAYER

Today our society is characterized by a great sense of narcissism or self-centeredness. This preoccupation with one's self results in excluding from our minds and hearts the true needs and concerns of others.

—Fr. Andrew Apostoli, *Soul Magazine*, Winter 2018

Read

Advent is a marvelous time to be more proactive with our works of charity. Certainly, this may seem countercultural while many around us are getting sucked into the widespread shopping frenzy. Our Lord calls us to perform works of charity. In the Gospel of Matthew, Jesus said, "Whatever you did to the least of my brothers, you did to me" (see Matt. 25:40). We are to serve Jesus in our neighbor, especially within the "least," the unfortunate. Our Lady of Fatima stressed the need for sacrifices for sinners. The year prior to Our Lady of Fatima's apparitions, the Angel of Peace appeared to the shepherd children and asked for sacrifices, and the children became more generous in their prayers and sacrifices. One time, the Angel of Peace brought the Eucharist to the three young shepherd children and taught them this prayer:

Most Holy Trinity—Father, Son, and Holy Spirit—I adore Thee profoundly. I offer Thee the most precious Body, Blood, Soul, and Divinity of Jesus Christ, present in all the tabernacles of the world, in reparation for the outrages, sacrileges, and indifferences whereby He is offended. And through the infinite merits of his Most Sacred Heart and the Immaculate Heart of Mary, I beg of Thee the conversion of poor sinners.

The Blessed Mother taught the children to offer personal sacrifices for the conversion of sinners with another prayer that became known as the Sacrifice Prayer:

O my Jesus, I offer this for love of Thee, for the conversion of sinners, and in reparation for the sins committed against the Immaculate Heart of Mary.

Fr. Andrew pointed out in the passage above that today's society is often navel gazing. Many are focused on pleasing and taking care of themselves. Fr. Andrew wrote, "We need to break from this self-focus by a spirit of sacrifice." In other words, it's about time for us to roll up our sleeves and start doing something for others. Our Lady of Fatima has asked for that. She has requested our sacrifices and prayers to help others. We need to get into the prayerful habit of performing works of mercy and charity.

As well, we live at a time when many have lost their faith, some do not know God at all, and others even hate God. The faithful can do their part to pray for all of these people. Fr. Andrew stated in an interview with the *National Catholic Register*:

Many have the notion that we don't need God, but we do. The threat of total war is very real. Our Lady promised an era of peace. That's why we must do what she told us in numbers great enough to bring about the conversion of the hearts of those who hate God. This will lead to the promised triumph of Mary's Immaculate Heart. At Fatima Mary was particularly concerned with the salvation of souls. She told the visionaries that many souls are lost from God because there is no one to pray and offer sacrifices for them.[10]

---

[10] Joseph Pronechen, "Fatima for Today," *National Catholic Register*, April 11, 2011.

Friday

We recall that Mary showed the faithful children a frightening vision of hell that remained etched upon their hearts, prodding them to make amends for sinners by praying and sacrificing for them. They dedicated the remainder of their lives to working tirelessly to save souls.

Fr. Andrew often stressed that Fatima is the most significant Church-approved apparition and that by following Our Lady's instructions we will help others and grow in holiness. He said, "Pope John Paul II said Fatima was the greatest apparition of the twentieth century and perhaps all time. Our Lady called her children to live holy lives of prayer and penance. This is missing in many people's lives today. They reject sacrifice because they're attached to the world and so cannot allow Jesus into their lives. If we follow what Our Lady is asking, we will find ourselves close to Jesus."[11] Following Fr. Andrew's instructions, we must pray and sacrifice so that those attached to the allurements, false promises, and sins of the world will recognize the web that has ensnared them.

About four months before Fr. Andrew left this world for his eternal reward, he said, "As you look around the world, some things seem a little bit hopeless. We are not going to stop this threat of war by having bigger nuclear weapons to blow each other off the face of the earth. But, Mary said, if people do as I have said, my victory will come — my triumph. And that will bring peace into the world. So we have to do what Our Lady asks."[12] Let us pray for a spirit of loving sacrifice so that we may help those around us who are struggling in some way. Mother Mary needs our help.

[11] Ibid.
[12] Andrew Apostoli, Holy Hour Lecture at the Thirtieth Annual Polish Walking Pilgrimage (2017).

WEEK 1: HOPE

Reflect

During this Advent, and especially today, try to be more generous with works of mercy. Your loving efforts can help to transform someone's life as well as your own soul! Be sure to prepare your heart for the upcoming Nativity of Our Lord Jesus, as well as for His Second Coming. Can you turn to the Blessed Mother often to ask for her help and graces? Try hard to schedule regular times for prayer and meditation each day and don't be concerned if you get interrupted by those who need you. That is your prayer in action—a work of mercy! Pick up where you left off after that. Ponder sacrifices you can make to offer in reparation for sinners.

Pray

Dear Jesus, please help me to commit more wholeheartedly to following Our Lady of Fatima's requests this Advent and beyond. Our Lady of Fatima, please pray for me.

*Pray the Rosary today in honor of Our Lady
of Fatima and for peace in the world.*

Act

Offer a sacrifice in reparation for sinners, as Our Lady of Fatima has asked. Perform at least one work of mercy. Strive to convert your heart today with God's grace and Mother Mary's help, remembering that conversion of heart should be a daily occurrence.

SATURDAY

FR. ANDREW OFFERS THE ULTIMATE SACRIFICIAL GIFT

Our Lady herself encouraged the children to pray the Rosary every day. When we pray the Rosary, we are being formed in the methods of prayer … vocal, then mental prayer, and finally affective prayer.

—Fr. Andrew Apostoli, *Soul Magazine*, Winter 2018

Read

The hundredth anniversary year of the apparitions of Our Lady of Fatima was a very meaningful and exceptional year for Fr. Andrew Apostoli. In addition to his preaching on Our Lady of Fatima and his television and radio shows, Fr. Andrew turned seventy-five and, on March 16, 2017, celebrated his golden jubilee — the fiftieth anniversary of his ordination to the priesthood. He also marked a thirty-year milestone in the founding of the Franciscan Friars of the Renewal. Still later that year, on December 13, Fr. Andrew closed his eyes to this world and the loved ones encircling his bed. Father passed on to his eternal reward with a peaceful last breath during the Litany of the Saints prayed by his fellow friars who were keeping vigil.

This humble friar had been filled with love and zeal to spread the gospel and, by God's grace, to help save as many souls as possible, which he worked at tirelessly — to the very end. At one point, Fr. Andrew shared what he believed was the authentic meaning of the priesthood, according to his "father in Christ," Venerable Fulton Sheen. He explained, "The image of the priesthood was that we had to be priest and victim with Christ. This is the meaning of the Christian priesthood. Fulton Sheen said that in the Christian priesthood what is unique is that we offer ourselves. We are both priest and victim."[13] Fr. Andrew wholeheartedly lived his vocation as a priest and victim with Christ. Throughout his priestly vocation, he stayed close to the Crucified Lord. Certainly, Mother Mary led the way for Fr. Andrew, who was so devoted to her. She, who was unconditionally faithful all the way to the Cross and beyond, was a vibrant holy example to Fr. Andrew.

Despite being stricken with a number of serious illnesses in his last year, Fr. Andrew was able to do some traveling for preaching and even managed to go to Fatima a couple of times. Unbeknownst to all but a few, though, Fr. Andrew wanted to do something special during that most significant year. He offered Our Lord and Our Lady of Fatima the ultimate gift. Father asked God for whatever cross he should receive. He wanted it all in order to save souls. He trusted that he would receive all necessary graces but knew it would certainly be difficult. There was no question there. Yet, as he gave his gift during that anniversary year, Father did not know that it would cost him his life here on earth. Yet, through his heroic surrender, he received eternal life in heaven.

Fr. Andrew suffered much through his illnesses. He had no idea how fast his decline would come. For a while, it looked as if he would get better. We were all very surprised, until we got closer to the end, when we realized that it wouldn't be much longer. Then, on the morning of December 13, Fr. Andrew lay sleeping in his bed, a rosary in his hands and a statue of Our Lady of Fatima nearby. His friars were all around him, praying the prayers for the dying. As Fr. Luke Fletcher shared with me, our dear Fr. Andrew breathed his last breath as they prayed the Litany of the Saints. Specifically, it was just after they called

---

[13] Pronechen, "Father Apostoli on Archbishop Sheen."

out, "St. Andrew, pray for us." Right before that, he had opened his eyes wide and apparently saw something that no one else there could see. I have no doubt that now, in his eternal reward, Father's vision is as clear as can be.

After Fr. Andrew's passing, Fr. Glenn Sudano, CFR, a fellow founding father reminisced, "He was very calming and very clear, easy to follow and soothing—not just on the ear, but on the soul." He added, "He had deep devotion and deep knowledge." Father Sudano explained, "He was able to articulate the faith in a very simple way and spoke to people in very Capuchin 'blue-collar preaching,' certainly always speaking the truth with a certain clarity—and always charity."[14]

Fr. Andrew would often discover spiritual lessons in the details and experiences of life. He was once leaving a St. Francis exhibit at the Metropolitan Museum of Art in New York when a poor, homeless man sitting on the steps asked him a startling question: "Are you for real or part of the show?" Father took it to heart and shared the story with the Missionaries of Charity Sisters, whom he served with Masses and teachings. He said that that unexpected question caused him to examine his motives and life. He instructed the Sisters to do the same. One of the Sisters reassured a reporter during an interview, "He was totally for real. He was 100% authentic and a great Friar for the renewal."[15]

I am blessed to have known such a wonderful friend who has been an amazing example of holiness to me. I thank God for this blessing, and I wish to pass along to others what I have learned from him. We shared many holy conversations over the years

---

[14] "Father Andrew Apostoli Remembered as a Bright Beacon of Light," *National Catholic Register*, December 15, 2017.
[15] Ibid.

and have prayed for each other. Father gave me many lengthy blessings, often over the phone, asking the Blessed Mother to place her holy mantle of protection upon me. I now ask Fr. Andrew each day to pray for my family and me, as well as for the many needs of others. I am confident that he hears my prayers. We are all a part of the Communion of Saints, after all.

I'll never forget our last conversation this side of heaven. I vividly recall visiting Fr. Andrew in his final days. My husband, Dave, and I were blessed that Fr. Andrew was strong enough for our visit. I brought some items for Father to bless and gave him a small statue of Our Lady of Fatima which, since his passing, I now cherish in my home. During our visit, Father sat in a wheelchair in the library with us, and we delved deeply into the saints and divine mercy, among other things. We had no idea at the time that dear Fr. Andrew would leave this life just a few weeks later. We were still hoping and praying for him to get better, if it was God's holy will.

Finally, parting at the door, after one more hug for the road, Fr. Andrew asked a nearby friar to close the door, which had been opened for our departure. He wanted to tell me something more. I knelt near him to be at his level in his wheelchair. Father said he appreciated our discussion and that it made him feel much better. My heart is happy knowing that I helped my saintly friend.

"We are both priest and victim," Fr. Andrew explained. Yes, dear Fr. Andrew offered himself as a victim—in full surrender to God's holy will—no matter how inconvenient or how very painful that would be. He did not know what lay before him, yet he trusted. He asked for the cross because he wanted to help save as many souls as possible. He wanted to help our Mother Mary. As I stated in an interview with the *National Catholic Register*, "Father Andrew was a bright beacon of light to our darkened world."[16] I have no doubt that he will continue to light the way for us to heaven.

With the prayer of St. Francis that Fr. Andrew offered to countless souls, I would like also to say, "May the Lord give you his peace."

Reflect

Take time to examine your life, as Fr. Andrew examined his. Are you ready to meet Our Lord? Each day we should be ready. Work hard at preparing your heart for the upcoming Nativity of Our Lord Jesus as well as for His Second Coming. Consider a sacrifice you can make to offer in reparation for sinners.

Pray

Our Lady of Fatima, please help me to be more cognizant of the state of my soul and changes I can make in my spiritual life this Advent to grow closer to your Son. Our Lady of Fatima, please pray for me.

Pray the Rosary today in honor of Our Lady of Fatima and for peace in the world.

Act

Offer a sacrifice in reparation for sinners, as Our Lady of Fatima has asked. Strive to convert your heart today with God's grace and Mother Mary's help, remembering that conversion of heart should be a daily occurrence.

[16] Ibid.

Week 2: Peace

THE SHEPHERD CHILDREN ILLUSTRATE FATIMA'S MESSAGE OF CONSOLING PEACE

Continue to pray the Rosary every day.

—Our Lady of Fatima to Sr. Lucia dos Santos

On this Second Sunday of Advent, we light our second Advent-wreath candle. It represents peace! Strive to live your Faith fully alive with peace during this week of Advent. This week we will look at Advent with Our Lady of Fatima at our side and through the eyes and hearts of the three young visionaries Lucia dos Santos, St. Francisco Marto, and his sister St. Jacinta Marto.

THE ANGEL OF PORTUGAL AND OUR LADY GUIDE US TO PEACE

My impression is that the Rosary is of the greatest value not only according to the words of Our Lady of Fatima, but according to the effects of the Rosary one sees throughout history. My impression is that Our Lady wanted to give ordinary people, who might not know how to pray, this simple method of getting closer to God.

—Sr. Lucia dos Santos

Read

The Blessed Mother's great love and concern for her children was displayed in her appearances to the three young shepherd children at Fatima. Our Lady came down from heaven to give the world a warning and to plead for prayers from the faithful.

Lucia dos Santos, the oldest of the three visionaries of the apparitions, became the spokesperson for the three children. As the apparitions unfolded, Lucia would also become a spokesperson for Our Lady to the world. It all began in Fatima, Portugal, in 1916, when the Angel of Portugal who was the Angel of Peace appeared to Lucia and her younger cousins, Francisco and Jacinta. The angel was sent from heaven to prepare the children's hearts for what was to come the following year. The angel quickly put the children's minds at ease and instructed them to make reparation for those who had offended God. Through a series of three visits, the radiant angel taught the children special prayers, including an intercessory prayer, and impressed upon their little hearts the great importance of praying to make up for the sins of the world. The angel also prepared them for the suffering they would later endure. Each visit brought additional teaching, culminating in the third teaching, which included Adoration of the Blessed Sacrament and the reception of Holy Communion from the angel.

Later, the Blessed Mother appeared to the faithful peasant children to entrust them with a powerful mission. Our Lady of Fatima first appeared to the unsuspecting shepherds on May 13, 1917, while they were out in the field grazing their sheep. It was at the Cova da Iria (or Cove of Irene, which means "peace") that the children were startled by unexpected flashes of light. Suddenly, a beautiful radiant Lady dressed in white stood on a nearby holm oak tree. The children learned right away in this first apparition that the Lady was from heaven, though they did not yet know that she was the Blessed Mother. The beautiful Lady told the children not to be afraid and spoke to them about heaven. Lucia spoke up and asked what the Lady wanted of her and eventually asked her if she and her cousins would go to heaven.

The children learned from the Lady that a friend who had died was in purgatory being purified. They knew that purgatory was not a punishment as much as it was a gift of mercy from God. They also were happy to learn that they would all go to heaven. Mary then asked the children if they would accept a holy mission.

> Are you willing to offer yourselves to God and bear all the sufferings He wills to send you, as an act of reparation for the sins by which He is offended, and of supplication for the conversion of sinners?[17]

They happily agreed, even though they were unaware of what was in store. Indeed, they must have received graces to accept the great calling. We should be inspired and deeply edified to know that these three young children were willing to do

---

[17] *Fatima, in Lucia's Own Words,* 158.

whatever it took to carry out the heavenly mission. This Advent, let us strive to offer our hearts completely to God.

Our Lady also told the children: "Pray the Rosary every day to obtain peace in the world, and an end to war." Lucia, Francisco, and Jacinta wholeheartedly agreed with the Blessed Mother's requests to accept the suffering that would come their way and to pray the Rosary every day. As faithful Catholic children, they had been praying the daily Rosary out in the fields after they ate their lunches, but, being so eager to play their games, they had rushed through the prayer. After Our Lady of Fatima requested the daily Rosary, they decided to oblige her with servant prayers, no longer rushing.

Lucia became a nun when she was older—first in the Dorothean Congregation and later in the Carmelite Order. In the passage that begins this chapter, Sr. Lucia reflects upon the great value and effects of the Rosary, based on what the Blessed Mother had told her and on her own observations. She considered that the Blessed Mother gave this "ordinary" way of prayer to folks so that they could grow closer to God. As a Carmelite nun, Sr. Lucia stated, "All people of good will can and must say the Rosary every day." She said it was "in order to put ourselves in contact with God, to thank Him for his benefits, and [to] ask for the graces we need. It is the prayer which places us in familiar contact with God, like the son who goes to his father to thank him for the gifts he has received, to talk to him about special concerns, to receive his guidance, his help, his support, and his blessing."[18]

---

[18] Joseph Pronechen, "Fatima's Sister Lucia Explains That Daily Rosary Is a Must," Eternal Word Television Network News, http://www.ewtnireland.com/fatimas-sister-lucia-explains-daily-rosary-must/.

WEEK 2: PEACE

Sr. Lucia explained that God requests "a prayer which is within our reach: the Rosary, which can be recited either in common or in private, either in church in the presence of the Blessed Sacrament or at home, either when traveling or while walking quietly in the fields. A mother of a family can say the Rosary while she rocks her baby's cradle or does the house work." She also explained why we should not have an excuse for not praying the Rosary daily. "Our day has 24 hours in it. It is not asking a great deal to set aside a quarter of an hour for the spiritual life, for our intimate and familiar converse with God."[19] Further, she tenderly said, "Those who pray the Rosary daily are like children who, every day, manage to find a few moments just to be with their father. It is an exchange of love. It is a mutual giving."[20]

Reflect

Our Lady of Fatima asked that the daily Rosary be prayed for peace in the world. Consider for a moment whether you make excuses for not praying the Rosary daily. Can you commit to trying to pray it daily? The three young shepherd children prayed the Rosary faithfully. As well, during this Advent, prepare your heart for the upcoming Nativity of Our Lord Jesus as well as for His Second Coming. Try to spend less time on media and television to pray the Rosary. In addition to the Rosary, schedule at least twenty minutes of prayer and meditation each day. Pray about a sacrifice you can make to offer in reparation for sinners.

[19] Ibid.
[20] "The Rosary Makes Possible an Intimate Relationship with God," The World Apostolate of Fatima, March 21, 2018, https://www.bluearmy.com/rosary-makes-possible-intimate-relationship-god/.

Sunday

This might sound like a lot to accomplish, but with God's amazing grace and the beautiful example of the shepherd children, you can do it!

Pray

Dear Jesus and Our Lady of Fatima, please help me to pray a fervent Rosary each day this Advent. Our Lady of Fatima, please pray for me.

Pray the Rosary today in honor of Our Lady of Fatima and for peace in the world.

Act

Offer a sacrifice in reparation for sinners, as Our Lady of Fatima has asked. Strive to convert your heart today with God's grace and Mother Mary's help, remembering that conversion of heart should be a daily occurrence.

RIDICULED LUCIA OVERCOMES DOUBT AND ACCEPTS GOD'S WILL

Let us all willingly endeavor to follow faithfully the path that He has mapped out for us. Yes, because it was out of love that God sent us this pressing call from his mercy, to help us along the way of our salvation.

—Sr. Lucia dos Santos[21]

[21] Philip Kosloski, "7 Powerful quotes from Fatima visionary Sister Lucia," Aleteia, February 16, 2017, https://aleteia. org/2017/02/16/7-powerful-quotes-from-fatima-visionary-sister-lucia/.

Read

We are already into the second week of a very holy season. Let's step back about one hundred years and get a feel for the mood of the people during those turbulent days. Throughout 1917, when the three shepherd children received enriching, informative, and holy visits from the Blessed Mother, not everyone was pleased. Many townspeople were upset, thinking the children were fabricating the story, and others were very skeptical. Yet many wanted to believe that the visits were truly from heaven. They had been craving peace in their lives, and they desired some good news for a change. At that time, many of the citizens, shepherds, and farmers were completely worn down by the devastation of the Great War. Their faith was shaken. That's when Our Lady of Fatima stepped in to rouse the lamenting village. The Queen of Heaven left her throne in heaven to bring amazing good news. Throughout her visits, the Blessed Mother delivered a magnificent message of hope—a long-hungered-for promise of peace. This assurance was not exclusively for the village of Fatima, though. It was meant for the whole world.

To deliver Our Lady of Fatima's message of the necessity of conversion of heart, prayer, sacrifice for sinners, and the ultimate promise of peace, Lucia, Francisco, and Jacinta had to experience and endure many sufferings and trials. They had agreed to

accept all the sufferings that God would allow to make reparation for sinners who had offended God. One of the sufferings the
children would endure was that they were not believed. They
were mocked and ridiculed by many, including members of their
own family.

This suffering was especially difficult for Lucia, whose
mother was one of those who were upset over the apparitions.
Perhaps "upset" is not a strong enough word to describe stern
Maria Rosa's sentiments about her daughter claiming to have
seen a Lady from heaven in a remote pasture, asking for specific
things. Maria Rosa was, in fact, angry when she first heard the
news. She feared embarrassment for the whole family and was
deeply concerned that Lucia was allowing the devil to play
tricks on her, or even worse, that Lucia was lying. In addition,
Lucia's siblings poked fun at her, which made it all the harder
on the ten-year-old. Maria Rosa arranged for her daughter to
meet with the parish priest to reveal what she had seen and
experienced, hoping that he would put an end to her nonsense.
But, after listening attentively to Lucia, Fr. Manuel Ferreira ad-
vised Maria Rosa to be patient and to wait and see what would
unfold.

The interrogations and lack of belief by so many wearied
Lucia. She began to experience doubts herself about whether the
devil was deceiving her, overwhelming her before it was time
to go back to the Cova da Iria to see the Lady for the second
apparition. But, throughout it all, the young visionary offered up
her sufferings and pain to God for the conversion of sinners. She
accepted the difficulties as part of God's plan and to keep her
promise to Mother Mary. God granted her the grace to go back
to the apparition site with her young cousins to become enlight-
ened by the remainder of the Blessed Mother's critical historic
messages.

Even though Lucia's mother was exceedingly hard on her daughter and at times used a broom shank on her for punishment, Lucia loved her mother and would later sing her praises for being a wonderful teacher of the Faith. She said, "My mother was a saint." She recalled how her Faith lessons affected her. "They were absorbed into my spirit and stored away in my memory, so much so that today I remember them with an intense longing for those happy times when innocence takes in and stores up everything as happy memories for later times."[22]

In the quote that begins our reflection today, we see that Lucia points out that God has a specific plan that is mapped out for us and that we should try hard to follow it faithfully. This is what Lucia did even as a young child. She might not have realized fully when she was young that faithfully and wholeheartedly following God's holy will would bring peace. During this holy season of Advent, we, too, can find peace as we try hard to follow God's holy will in our lives.

Reflect

There will be times when we are not believed, or when we will be ridiculed for our Faith. How will we respond? Will it be with patience and resignation to the will of God? Will we grow from the experience and pray for grace? In recalling Lucia's memories of her mother's Faith lessons and her longing for "those happy times," and remembering that young children are impressionable and open to learning the Faith, can you be sure to be a wonderful, holy influence on all the young ones in your life? As you navigate through this holy season, be sure to prepare your heart for the upcoming Nativity of Our Lord Jesus, as well as for

[22] Fr. Robert J. Fox, *The Intimate Life of Sister Lucia* (Hanceville, AL: Fatima Family Apostolate, n.d.), 65.

His Second Coming. Ponder sacrifices you can make to offer in reparation for sinners, as Our Lady of Fatima has asked.

Pray

Dear Jesus and Our Lady of Fatima, please help me to be open to God's holy will for my life this Advent. Help me also to pray for those who belittle me or criticize me in any way. Grant me the graces to teach the Faith to the young and old alike in my life. Our Lady of Fatima, please pray for me.

Pray the Rosary today in honor of Our Lady of Fatima and for peace in the world.

Act

Offer a sacrifice in reparation for sinners, as Our Lady of Fatima has asked. Strive to convert your heart today with God's grace and Mother Mary's help, remembering that conversion of heart should be a daily occurrence.

TUESDAY

ST. FRANCISCO FINDS PEACE
IN THE "HIDDEN JESUS"

God's presence became constant in their lives, as is evident from their insistent prayers for sinners and their desire to remain ever near "the hidden Jesus" in the tabernacle.

—Pope Francis at the canonization of
St. Francisco and St. Jacinta

Read

Let's look at how a simple peasant farm boy overcame opposition and suffering: Little Francisco ran to his "hidden Jesus" in the Blessed Sacrament whenever he could. Jesus' presence in the Eucharist is central to our Faith and to the message of Our Lady of Fatima.

The Angel of Peace taught the shepherd children about adoration of Jesus in the Blessed Sacrament during his third visit with them. It was in the fall of 2016. The children were praying with their heads bowed to the ground, as the angel had taught them, while their sheep grazed nearby. A sudden flash of light got their attention and they saw that the radiant angel was back. He was holding a beautiful chalice in his left hand, and a Eucharistic Host hovered above it. Distinct red drops of Jesus' Precious Blood dripped down from the Host and fell into the chalice. The children were amazed and took it all in. Suddenly, the Angel of Peace left the Host and the chalice hovering in the air and knelt with the children. Along with Lucia, Francisco, and Jacinta, the angel adored Jesus in the Blessed Sacrament. He demonstrated to the children that we do not worship angels; we worship God alone. They all put their foreheads to the ground and reverently prayed a prayer that the angel had taught the children:

WEEK 2: PEACE

Most Holy Trinity, Father, Son, and Holy Spirit, I adore
You profoundly, and I offer You the most Precious Body,
Blood, Soul, and Divinity of Jesus Christ, present in all
the tabernacles of the world, in reparation for the outrages, sacrileges, and indifference with which He Himself
is offended. And through the infinite merits of his Most
Sacred Heart, and the Immaculate Heart of Mary, I beg
you the conversion of poor sinners.[23]

They prayed this together three times. After that, the Angel
gave Holy Communion to the peasant children. It would be
Francisco and Jacinta's First Holy Communion—given by an
Angel! After some time, the Angel departed, and the children
remained in prayer, enveloped within God's mysterious and
holy graces. They were deeply impacted by the Angel's visit, as
well as receiving the Body and Blood of Jesus. After this visit,
all three firmly committed to pray hard and do all they could to
make reparation for sinners who have offended God.

In an earlier visit, the Angel of Peace taught the children the
following intercessory prayer, which speaks of adoring Jesus:

My God, I believe, I adore, I hope, and I love You! I beg
pardon for those who do not believe, do not adore, do not
hope, and do not love You.

It is essential for Catholics to show their love to God
through prayer and adoration of the Blessed Sacrament, in
which Jesus is truly present—Body, Blood, Soul, and Divinity.
The Angel of Peace taught the children simple, foundational,
and powerful lessons, in preparation for the Virgin Mary's amazing miraculous visits the following year, in 1917. Clearly, the

---

[23] Lucia dos Santos, *Fatima, in Lucia's Own Words*, 152.

three young visionaries were chosen by God to learn great truths of the Faith and to pass them on to the world through their surrender and commitment to following God's holy will.

All the children became holy and devoted to the Blessed Sacrament, but Francisco was particularly drawn to his "hidden Jesus." He much preferred being with Jesus in the quiet of St. Anthony's church than anywhere else. Whenever he had the chance, he would steal away to the "hidden Jesus" to pray earnestly, pouring out his innocent childlike love to Jesus.

St. John Paul II spoke about Francisco Marto and his sister, Jacinta, at their beatification Mass. He spoke about Francisco's loving heart and his desire to console Jesus, which we will get to in a later chapter. As well, at Fatima, Pope Francis mentioned the hidden Jesus at St. Francisco's and St. Jacinta's canonizations. He said, "We can take as our examples St. Francisco and St. Jacinta, whom the Virgin Mary introduced into the immense ocean of God's light and taught to adore him." He explained, "That was the source of their strength in overcoming opposition and suffering. God's presence became constant in their lives, as is evident from their insistent prayers for sinners and their desire to remain ever near 'the hidden Jesus' in the tabernacle."[24] We can certainly learn about the importance of our prayers in Adoration of Jesus from little Francisco, now a saint of our Church. Let us never tire of visiting sweet Jesus, awaiting us in the tabernacle. We may not have a whole hour, but whatever time we can carve from our schedule will indeed bring peace into our lives.

---

[24] The Divine Mercy, "Pope Francis in Fatima Canonizes Shepherd Children," Marians of the Immaculate Conception, May 13, 2017, https://www.thedivinemercy.org/news/Pope-in-Fatima-Canonizes-Shepherd-Children-7209.

WEEK 2: PEACE

Reflect

Take a few moments to reflect on your love for Jesus in the Blessed Sacrament. It may not be easy to get to a chapel or to a church, but do your best to make additional visits to Him, even for ten or fifteen minutes here and there, throughout this grace-filled season of Advent. These visits will help you to prepare your heart for the Nativity of Our Lord Jesus as well as for His Second Coming. Jesus in the Blessed Sacrament will surely fill your heart with the necessary grace and peace to navigate this busy season.

Pray

Our Lady of Fatima, please help me to commit to additional time visiting Jesus in the Blessed Sacrament this Advent. Inspire my heart to make amends and offer sacrifices for the conversion of sinners, as the Fatima visionaries did. Our Lady of Fatima, please pray for me.

*Pray the Rosary today in honor of Our Lady
of Fatima and for peace in the world.*

Act

Offer a sacrifice in reparation for sinners, as Our Lady of Fatima has asked. Strive to convert your heart today with God's grace and Mother Mary's help, if possible while with Jesus in the Blessed Sacrament, remembering that conversion of heart should be a daily occurrence.

FROM FEAR TO PEACE: THE SHEPHERD CHILDREN SAVE SINNERS FROM HELL

Pray! Pray a great deal and make many sacrifices, for many souls go to hell because they have no one to make sacrifices and to pray for them.

—Our Lady of Fatima to St. Jacinta,
St. Francisco, and Sr. Lucia

Read

Let's now look at the second apparition of Our Lady of Fatima, in July 2017, when the Blessed Mother showed Lucia, Francisco, and Jacinta a haunting vision of hell with all its frightening details. For a moment, the children stood frozen in fear. The Virgin Mary found it necessary to show the three innocent children the reality of hell. She would also tell them that many are sent to hell because there is no one to pray for them. She asked them to pray and make sacrifices to help convert sinners.

In his theological commentary on the message of Fatima, written when he was Joseph Cardinal Ratzinger, Pope Emeritus Benedict XVI provides a wonderful interpretation of the purpose of the vision of hell in the lives of the children, and he ties in Mary's Immaculate Heart, St. Paul, and Jesus. He says:

> For one terrible moment, the children were given a vision of hell. They saw the fall of "the souls of poor sinners." And now they are told why they have been exposed to this moment: "in order to save souls"—to show the way to salvation. The words of the First Letter of Peter come to mind: "As the outcome of your faith you obtain the salvation of your souls" (1:9). To reach this goal, the way indicated … is devotion to the Immaculate Heart of Mary.

WEEK 2: PEACE

A brief comment may suffice to explain this. In biblical language the "heart" indicates the center of human life, the point where reason, will, temperament and sensitivity converge, where the person finds his unity and his interior orientation. According to Matthew 5:8, the "immaculate heart" is a heart which makes the *fiat*—"your will be done"—the defining center of one's whole life. It might be objected that we should not place a human being between ourselves and Christ. But then we remember that Paul did not hesitate to say to his communities: "imitate me" (1 Cor. 4:16; Phil. 3:17; 1 Thess. 1:6; 2 Thess. 3:7, 9). In the Apostle they could see concretely what it meant to follow Christ. But from whom might we better learn in every age than from the Mother of the Lord?[25]

After witnessing the horrifying vision, the three visionaries did not want anyone to have to suffer the eternal fate of hell! Sweet Jacinta would often cry out, "Oh, hell! Hell! How sorry I am for the souls who go to hell! And the people down there, burning alive, like wood in the fire!"[26] All three cousins stepped up their prayers and sacrifices for sinners. They became passionate about saving souls. Just before Francisco's death, Jacinta told him, according to Pope John Paul II at the beatification Mass, "Give my greetings to Our Lord and to Our Lady and tell them that I am enduring everything they want for the conversion of

---

[25] Congregation for the Doctrine of the Faith, "The Message of Fatima," http://www.vatican.va/roman_curia/congregations/cfaith/documents/rc_con_cfaith_doc_20000626_message-fatima_en.html.

[26] Lucia Maria and Luís Kondor, *Fatima in Lucia's Own Words: Sister Lucia's Memories* (Fatima, Portugal: Postulation Centre, 1976), 105.

sinners." Little Jacinta's passionate commitment to saving souls surely must have warmed Our Lord's and Our Lady's hearts!

Certainly, hell is not a happy subject, and perhaps it is a very uncomfortable one. Lucia would later say as a nun that many people are hesitant to talk about hell, especially to children. Specifically, she said, "Some people, even the most devout, refuse to speak to children about hell, in case it would frighten them. Yet God did not hesitate to show hell to three children, one of whom was only six years old, knowing well that they would be horrified to the point of ... withering away with fear."[27] Indeed, we are in this world to work out our salvation—day by day, right within the nitty gritty details of life. We need to prepare our hearts and souls for the next life. Our example and prayers can truly help others to see the reality of eternal life. We should never hesitate to talk about the reality of hell whenever the opportunity presents itself. That conversation could very well help someone to desire to convert his heart and turn to God before it is too late.

Reflect

Our Lady of Fatima asked the shepherd children to pray much and make many sacrifices for the conversion of sinners. Even small sacrifices offered lovingly to God can make a difference. The Angel of Peace told the children:

> Make of everything you can a sacrifice and offer it to God as an act of reparation for the sins by which He is offended, and in supplication for the conversion of sinners. You will thus draw down peace upon your country. I am its Angel Guardian, the Angel of Portugal. Above all, accept and bear with submission the suffering which the Lord will send you.

[27] Ibid.

WEEK 2: PEACE

From these instructions we learn that we can use "everything" to make a sacrifice. We should have no excuses!

Get into the habit of offering everything you can for the love of God, for the conversion of sinners, and for reparation for the sins committed against Mary's Immaculate Heart. All the while, prepare your heart for Jesus' coming at Christmas and for His Second Coming, because Advent has a twofold meaning. We need to stay awake!

Pray

Dear Jesus and Our Lady of Fatima, thank you for the knowledge of eternal life. Help me to help others this Advent and beyond, mindful that many do not believe that hell exists or that there is a punishment for sin. Our Lady of Fatima, please pray for me.

Pray the Rosary today in honor of Our Lady of Fatima and for peace in the world.

Act

Our Lady of Fatima taught the following Sacrifice Prayer to the children. She asked them to pray it often.

O Jesus, it is for love of You, for the conversion of sinners, and in reparation for the sins committed against the Immaculate Heart of Mary.[28]

Try to make more sacrifices in reparation and pray this prayer often. As well, strive to convert your heart today with God's grace and Mother Mary's help, remembering that conversion of heart should be a daily occurrence.

[28] Lucia dos Santos, *Fatima, in Lucia's Own Words*, 152.

THURSDAY

DEVOTION TO MARY'S
IMMACULATE HEART
BRINGS PEACE

I will never forsake you. My Immaculate Heart will be your refuge and the way that will lead you to God.

—Our Lady of Fatima to Lucia, June 13, 1917

Read

The assurance about going to heaven that Our Lady gave the children during her first visit thoroughly delighted them. Yet Lucia had a burning desire to go to heaven right away, so she ventured to ask Our Lady during the second visit, in June 1917, if she could take them to heaven. Our Lady let Lucia know that she would be taking Jacinta and Francisco soon, but that she (Lucia) would need to stay behind for a while longer. Lucia's future efforts were essential. It was because, as the Blessed Mother said, "Jesus wishes to make use of you to make me known and loved. He wants to establish in the world devotion to my Immaculate Heart." The strong familial bond to her younger cousins, who were also tied together in the mission of these marvelous heavenly apparitions, caused the Lady's answer to be bittersweet for Lucia. Lucia's eyes revealed to the Blessed Mother that she was hesitant to stay "alone" on earth while her cousins went to heaven. As well, the holy Lady knew her heart. That's when Mary reassured her that she would never forsake the young visionary. After presenting her Immaculate Heart, Mary also promised Lucia that her Immaculate Heart would be her refuge and would also lead Lucia to God.

The Blessed Mother reaffirmed her Immaculate Heart in the July apparition, after first showing the children the terrifying vision of hell we spoke about in the last chapter. She told the young visionaries that she desired a consecration to her Immaculate Heart as a means of conversion and reparation. As well, her request that Russia be consecrated to her Immaculate Heart emphasizes the need for devotion to the Heart of Mary. Later, in the visions that conclude the event of Fatima (at Pontevedra and Tuy) Mary again renewed the request for consecration that became associated with the Communion of Reparation on the Five First Saturdays.

So, why should we be devoted to Mary's Immaculate Heart? First, it is simply because she asks this of us. The Blessed Mother told the shepherd children, "To save the souls of poor sinners, God wishes to establish the devotion to my Immaculate Heart throughout the world." But, this was not the first time that Mary's Immaculate Heart came into the world. The devotion to Mary's Immaculate Heart has grown through the centuries and is said to have begun at the time of St. John Eudes, who was born in 1601 in Normandy, France. St. John worked tirelessly to teach people about the Hearts of Jesus and Mary. He composed Masses and Offices in honor of both Jesus and Mary and was responsible for the first Feast of the Holy Heart of Mary, celebrated on February 8, 1648, at Autun (France), and the Feast of the Heart of Jesus celebrated later, on October 20, 1672.

An article by the *Catholic News Agency* explains the differences between the Sacred Heart of Jesus and the Immaculate Heart of Mary and how one leads us to the other. "Devotion concerned with Jesus emphasizes his divine heart as being full of love for mankind, but with this love for the most part being ignored or rejected; in contrast, devotion to Mary's heart is essentially concerned with the love that her heart has for Jesus, for God." The article further explains, "It is not an end in itself, so the love of her heart is meant to be a model for the way we should love God. The fact that her heart is immaculate — that is, sinless — means that she is the only fully human person who is able to really love God in the way that he should be loved."[29]

It's important to note that while we love Mary, we do not worship her. We honor her with love and prayers and ask for her help. We worship God alone in His three Divine Persons: Father, Son, and Holy Spirit. Mary was chosen for the role of bringing our Savior Jesus Christ into the world. However, it didn't stop there. Mary stuck right by her Son all the way to the Cross — and beyond. She always cooperated with the graces bestowed upon her to do what heaven called her to do. Yet, it was necessary for her to move her will to do what was asked. In other words, she could have said no or could even have said yes and not followed through.

Mary is our wonderful intermediary. For instance, when we make a consecration to Jesus through Mary, we are worshiping Jesus and asking Mother Mary to help us make our consecration beautifully and sincerely. Everything Mary does will lead us to her Son Jesus. It's what mothers do, after all! When Lucia was a nun, she stated, "God began the work of our redemption in the Heart of Mary, given that it was through her 'fiat' that the redemption began to come about." These are wise words indeed.

Shortly before little Jacinta's death, she passionately reminded her older cousin Lucia of her grave responsibility. She said, "You must stay and tell people that God wants to establish in the world devotion to the Immaculate Heart of Mary." Jacinta

---

[29] "The Immaculate Heart of Mary," Catholic News Agency, https://www.catholicnewsagency.com/resources/mary/popular-marian-devotions/the-immaculate-heart-of-mary.

gave her older cousin a little pep talk and some wise advice: "When you have to say this, don't hide, but tell everybody that God gives us his grace through the Immaculate Heart of Mary and that people must ask it through her and that the Sacred Heart of Jesus wants the Immaculate Heart of Mary by his side. They must ask peace through the Immaculate Heart because God has given it to her."[30] Lucia would later state, "Thus we see that devotion to the Immaculate Heart of Mary must be established in the world by means of a true consecration, through conversion and self-giving."[31] Lucia's sage advice about conversion and self-giving can be put into practice this Advent!

Reflect

Young Lucia was concerned about being left behind when her younger cousins went to heaven. We recall that Mary reassured her that her Immaculate Heart would be her refuge as well as a way that would lead her to God. As well, through her apparitions, the Blessed Mother requested devotion to her Immaculate Heart. Take time to ponder and pray about your devotion to Mother Mary. Do you turn to her in your needs and ask her to help you draw closer to her Son? Can you? Get to know Mary better. Mary's Immaculate Heart will certainly bring comfort to your soul.

Pray

Our Lady of Fatima, please help me to draw closer to your Immaculate Heart and to the Sacred Heart of your Son

---

[30] John de Marchi, I.M.C., *Fatima: From the Beginning*, trans. I. M. Kingsbury (Fatima: Missoes Consolata Fatima, 2006), 192.
[31] Pronechen, "Fatima's Sister Lucia Explains That Daily Rosary Is a Must."

Thursday

Jesus during this Advent. Our Lady of Fatima, please pray for me and all whose lives I touch.

Pray the Rosary today in honor of Our Lady
of Fatima and for peace in the world.

Act

Offer a sacrifice (possibly taking a shorter shower or bath, getting up earlier in the morning, fasting from a pleasure) in reparation for sinners, as Our Lady of Fatima has asked. Strive to convert your heart today with God's grace and Mother Mary's help, remembering that conversion of heart should be a daily occurrence.

FRIDAY

THE FATIMA VISIONARIES
AND THE EUCHARIST

It is through the meditative prayer of adoration in front of the Blessed Sacrament that the Kingdom of God will come to earth, transforming the lives of our entire societies as they come closer to God.

— Prof. Américo Pablo López-Ortiz, International President of the World Apostolate of Fatima

Read

Moving closer to the end of the second week of Advent, we focus on the Eucharist. Jesus said, "I am the bread of life.... He who eats my flesh and drinks my blood abides in me and I in him. As I live because of the Father, so he who eats me will live because of me" (John 6:48, 56–57). The Eucharist is central to our lives as Catholics and, as discussed earlier, a vital part of Our Lady of Fatima's message. The shepherd children were instructed in the Eucharist. Let's look at what our Church teaches: "At the Last Supper, on the night he was betrayed, our Savior instituted the Eucharistic sacrifice of his Body and Blood. This he did in order to perpetuate the sacrifice of the cross throughout the ages until he should come again, and so to entrust to his beloved Spouse, the Church, a memorial of his death and resurrection: a sacrament of love, a sign of unity, a bond of charity, a Paschal banquet 'in which Christ is consumed, the mind is filled with grace, and a pledge of future glory is given to us.' "[32]

---

[32] *Catechism of the Catholic Church* (CCC), no. 1323, quoting Constitution on the Sacred Liturgy *Sacrosanctum concilium* (December 4, 1963), no. 47.

St. Irenaeus called the Eucharist, "The prolongation of the incarnation."[33] The Incarnation began in Christ's mother's womb. The Blessed Mother is intimately united to Jesus in the Eucharist. An eminent authority on the Eucharist, St. Peter Julian Eymard, who founded the Blessed Sacrament Fathers, gave Mary the title "Our Lady of the Most Blessed Sacrament." He stated, "It was her consent to the Incarnation of the Word in her womb that inaugurated the great mystery of reparation to God and union with us which Jesus accomplished during his mortal life; and He continues in the Eucharist."[34]

As a Carmelite nun, Sr. Lucia spoke about Mary's connection to the Eucharist. She said:

> It is the body received from Mary, that in Christ becomes a victim offered up for the salvation of mankind; it is the blood received from Mary that circulates in Christ's veins and which pours out from his Divine Heart; it is this same body and this same blood, received from Mary, that are given to us, under the appearances of bread and wine, as our daily food, to strengthen within us the life of grace, and so continue in us, members of the Mystical Body of Christ, his redemptive work for the salvation of each and all to the extent to which each one clings to Christ and co-operates with Christ.[35]

[33] Richard Nicholas, "The Significance of the Eucharist in the Apparitions at Fatima," *Homiletic and Pastoral Review* (December 2017), https://www.hprweb.com/2017/12/the-significance-of-the-eucharist-in-the-apparitions-at-fatima/.

[34] Ibid.

[35] Pronechen, "Fatima's Sister Lucia Explains That Daily Rosary Is a Must".

Friday

Amazingly, the children were catechized in the Eucharist by the Angel of Peace and Our Lady. We recall that at the first visit, the angel bowed profoundly and taught the poor shepherds this prayer: "My God, I believe, I adore, I hope, and I love You. I ask pardon for those who do not believe, do not adore, do not hope, and do not love You." In the second visit, he taught them to offer everything to God as a reparation for sin. In his third visit, he taught Lucia, Francisco, and little Jacinta how to adore Jesus in the Blessed Sacrament, and he also gave them Holy Communion, which underscores the great importance of Jesus in our lives and of nourishing our hearts and souls with the Bread of Life. Later, after the angel's visits, in 1917, the Mother of God would train the young visionaries through each of her apparitions. She taught Lucia, Francisco, and Jacinta how to worship and adore God.

The Church teaches:

> In the Eucharist the sacrifice of Christ becomes also the sacrifice of the members of his Body. The lives of the faithful, their praise, their suffering, their prayers, their work, are united to those of Christ. In as much as it is a sacrifice, the Eucharist is likewise offered for all the faithful, living and dead, in reparation for the sins of all and to obtain spiritual and temporal benefits from God. The Church in heaven is also united to the offering of Christ.[36]

As we learn from the three young children, adoring Jesus in the Blessed Sacrament is not reserved for adults. Prof. Américo Pablo López-Ortiz, international president of the World Apostolate of Fatima, spoke about the importance of teaching

---

[36] *Compendium of the Catechism of the Catholic Church*, no. 281.

children to pray in adoration. He spoke about hope for the future in our children and Our Lady of Fatima's message. He said, "There is a great sign of hope: Our Lady of Fatima revealed in her Apparitions the great role of children in our times in the Divine Plan for the salvation of many souls." He encourages us to recognize how wonderful things can happen with prayer — with children's innocent prayer, especially in front of the Blessed Sacrament. Specifically, he said, "when children come together to pray, as the three little shepherds of Fatima did in the first prayer cell of the world, great things happened. The formidable obstacles created by evil, hatred, and violence crumble as they are confronted with the pure, simple faith of children in God's love, grace, and mercy."

We must teach our children and grandchildren the message of Our Lady of Fatima, the importance of prayer and sacrifice for sinners, and encourage them to spend time with Jesus in the Blessed Sacrament. As Prof. López-Ortiz puts it, "Our children must come to our tabernacles to visit Jesus Christ present in a real way, waiting for them, to transform them into his image so that they will become light for the world, salt for their families, and happiness for our entire societies. It is through the meditative prayer of adoration in front of the Blessed Sacrament that the Kingdom of God will come to earth, transforming the lives of our entire societies as they come closer to God."[37]

Reflect

We can be sure that time with Jesus in the Blessed Sacrament in adoration and in receiving the Eucharist at Mass give us

---

[37] "Message from the international president of the World Apostolate of Fatima," Children of the Eucharist, https://childrenoftheeucharist.org/fatima-documents/.

much peace and the necessary strength to fight the good fight and make our way to heaven. We should strive to be with Jesus in His Eucharistic presence whenever we are able. We should also try to make more fervent thanksgivings after receiving Jesus in Holy Communion. During this Advent, draw closer to your Savior and prepare your heart for His coming at Christmas, as well as for His Second Coming. Stay awake!

Pray

Dear Jesus and Our Lady of Fatima, please help me to receive Holy Communion more worthily this Advent. Our Lady of Fatima, please pray for me.

Pray the Rosary today in honor of Our Lady of Fatima and for peace in the world.

ANIMA CHRISTI (SOUL OF CHRIST)
(Very fitting to pray after receiving Holy Communion)

Soul of Christ, sanctify me.
Body of Christ, save me.
Blood of Christ, inebriate me.
Water from Christ's side, wash me.
Passion of Christ, strengthen me.
O good Jesus, hear me.
Within Thy wounds hide me.
Suffer me not to be separated from Thee.
From the malicious enemy defend me.
In the hour of my death call me
and bid me come unto Thee
that I may praise Thee with Thy saints
and with Thy angels,
forever and ever. Amen.

WEEK 2: PEACE

Act

Draw closer to Jesus today. Offer a sacrifice in reparation for sinners, as Our Lady of Fatima has asked. Every sacrifice—big or small—when offered lovingly is pleasing to God. Strive to convert your heart today with God's grace and Mother Mary's help, remembering that conversion of heart should be a daily occurrence.

DIFFICULTIES AMID GRACE UNITE LUCIA TO THE CROSS OF CHRIST

What a beautiful ideal to be crucified with Christ!
That He may inebriate me with gladness of the Cross.
Here lies the secret of my happiness—not to want or
wish for more than to love and suffer for love.[38]

—Sr. Lucia

---

[38] Fox, *The Intimate Life of Sister Lucia*, 313.

Read

All three shepherd children gave their wholehearted fiats to the Blessed Mother on May 13, 1917, when she asked them, "Are you willing to offer yourselves to God and bear all the sufferings He wills to send you, as an act of reparation for the sins by which He is offended, and of supplication for the conversion of sinners?"[39] As soon as they agreed, Our Lady of Fatima warned them, "Then you are going to have much to suffer." But she reassured them, "But the grace of God will be your comfort."[40] The children's hearts had been prepared to give their yes to this great mission by the angel's visits and, later, through comfort from the beautiful heavenly Lady. The children did not yet realize how quickly their suffering would unfold. Yet they were willing to do what was necessary so that God's will could be accomplished.

Some of the suffering they would endure began with their parents and family, who were skeptical of their stories about seeing the Lady from heaven, especially Lucia's mother, who was angry at her. In time, the Dos Santoses' fields were ruined from the thousands of pilgrims who trudged across them to get to the

---

[39] *Fatima in Lucia's Own Words*, 158.
[40] Ibid.

Cova da Iria. Their crops had been a big part of their livelihood. Lucia's mother was livid. Ever since the first apparition of Our Lady of Fatima on May 13, 1917, and through October 13, the children were plagued by constant questioning, interrogation, and even abduction and time in jail. The authorities threatened to boil them in oil if they did not renounce the apparitions and reveal any secrets they had been told.

The children stayed true to their promises to the Lady. Not only that: when they were imprisoned, they were beautiful witnesses to the hardened criminals alongside them. Their example of kneeling, praying, and offering their suffering for the conversion of sinners and in reparation for the sins committed against the Immaculate Heart of Mary brought prisoners to their knees, and they prayed with the children. Finally, on August 15, the Solemnity of the Assumption of the Blessed Virgin Mary into heaven, the children were released, and Our Lady appeared to them a few days later. During this visit on August 19, Our Lady of Fatima told the children, "Pray, pray very much, and make sacrifices for sinners; for many souls go to hell because there are none to sacrifice themselves and pray for them."[41]

After Our Lady's pleading, Lucia, Francisco, and Jacinta prayed even harder to save souls. They devoted the rest of their lives to praying and sacrificing. Their example, as young children, of going without water on hot summer days out in the fields, and even wearing ropes around their waists under their clothing to bear a bit more pain, might put many of us adults to shame because of our lack of commitment or laziness. All three visionaries endured much pain and made many

---

[41] "The Revelations of the Two Hearts in Modern Times," EWTN, https://www.ewtn.com/library/mary/firstsat.htm.

sacrifices for sinners. Francisco persevered in prayer while his head was throbbing in pain during the illness that ultimately took his life. Little Jacinta, racked with pain in the hospital, told Our Lady yes when asked if she would stay on earth a little longer to save more souls. Lucia had been told by Our Lady that she would need to stay a while longer to carry out the message. This she did perseveringly through all sorts of pain and troubles in the convents. She had learned to read and write, as Our Lady asked: she worked very hard through many years, writing letters of encouragement to priests and seminarians, making rosaries, and humbly working diligently in the convent. Sr. Lucia, the oldest Fatima visionary, died at almost ninety-eight years of age.

When Sr. Lucia entered Carmel, she straightaway noticed a unique cross hanging on the wall of her new cell. She recounted the experience when in 1954 she wrote:

> When I had the good fortune of entering the Carmelite Order, I was led to the cell, and as I was entering it I fixed my eyes on the big stripped cross that opened its arms to me. Our Reverend Mother Prioress asked me: "Do you know why this cross has no statue [corpus]? And without giving me time to answer she added: "It is so that you may crucify yourself on it." What a beautiful ideal to be crucified with Christ! That He may inebriate me with gladness of the Cross. Here lies the secret of my happiness—not to want or wish for more than to love and suffer for love . . . [42]

Many are unaware that difficulties occur even in holy places—perhaps, most especially in those places. Our Lord, the

[42] Fox, *The Intimate Life of Sister Lucia*, 313.

Divine Physician, knows exactly what we need and when we need it. On December 29, 1955, Sr. Maria Lucia wrote to her Father Superior:

> Difficulties grow everywhere and that is why we need the help of divine grace to obtain something that is good. May Our Lady as a loving mother watch over us and help us all. The multitude of letters that arrive here from all over the world bear witness to this. They do little more than complain about the miseries that flood mankind. In view of this I become convinced that only myself and the little group, who as myself had the good fortune of consecrating themselves to Our Lord, are the only happy people on earth. It is not that one does not live without a cross, because this is part of being the chosen people. But if it is carried with love, it becomes a treasure of appreciable value, which in fact none of those who follow Christ wants to lose.
>
> I don't know if you have ever seen the cell of a Carmelite. In each cell there is a wooden cross without the statue. It is so that following the example of Jesus she should be crucified on it, to follow Him step by step to Calvary, where she must suffer and die with Him for love and for the souls that He may want to save through her. Looking this way at the cross, it becomes light and easy to carry; one loves because in it one finds knowledge of union with our God crucified for us, and one does not wish anything more than to love and suffer for love.[43]

---

[43] Ibid.

Saturday

Reflect

At the end of this second week of Advent, what can you learn from Our Lady and the three heroic children of Fatima? Are you praying very much, as Our Lady of Fatima asked the children? Can you submit your will wholeheartedly to the will of God? Can you embrace whatever He wants for you, including suffering? Will you look upon your crosses in life as Sr. Lucia has? She said that the cross becomes easy and light when we unite ourselves to Jesus on the Cross. Remember that Our Lady told the children that the grace of God will be their comfort. Take time to ponder and pray about this.

Pray

Dear Jesus and Our Lady of Fatima, please teach me to resign my will to God's will this Advent. Our Lady of Fatima, please pray for me.

*Pray the Rosary today in honor of Our Lady
of Fatima and for peace in the world.*

Act

Offer a sacrifice in reparation for sinners, as Our Lady of Fatima has asked. Strive to convert your heart today with God's grace and Mother Mary's help, remembering that conversion of heart should be a daily occurrence.

Week 3: Joy

THE JUBILANT JOY OF THE FATIMA MESSAGE WITH ST. JOHN PAUL II

To save the souls of poor sinners, God wishes to establish the devotion to my Immaculate Heart throughout the world.

—Our Lady of Fatima to St. Jacinta,
St. Francisco, and Sr. Lucia

O n this Third Sunday of Advent, which is called Gaudete Sunday, we light our third Advent-wreath candle. It represents joy! Strive to live your Faith fully alive with joy during this week of Advent. This week we will look at Advent with Our Lady of Fatima at our side and through the eyes and heart of St. John Paul II. St. John Paul II was one of the most beloved popes of the Catholic Church, and he had much to do with Fatima, as we shall read this week.

ST. JOHN PAUL II'S MYSTERIOUS CONNECTION TO FATIMA

Consecrating the world to the Immaculate Heart
of the Mother means returning beneath the cross
of the Son. It means consecrating this world to the
pierced heart of the Savior, bringing it back to the
very source of its redemption. Redemption is always
greater than man's sin and the "sin of the world."
The power of Redemption is infinitely superior to the
whole range of evil in man and the world. The heart
of Mary is aware of this, more than any other heart
in the whole universe, visible and invisible. And so
she calls us. She not only calls us to be converted: she
calls us to accept her motherly help to return to the
source of redemption.

—Pope St. John Paul II, Homily at Fatima, May 13, 1982

Read

Here we are beginning the third week of Advent. We are half-way through our Advent pilgrimage. There's still time to make better efforts! Let's begin this week by looking at our dearly beloved Polish pope. St. John Paul II was intimately connected to the message of Fatima. Actually, he was not just connected to it but was really a part of it! Let's back up to see how.

St. John Paul II was the first non-Italian pope in 455 years! He was very charismatic and beloved, and he led the Church into the new millennium. His great love for the Blessed Mother grew stronger after he read St. Louis-Marie Grignon de Montfort's book *True Devotion to Mary*. To reflect his devotion to Mary, he took for his motto *Totus tuus* ("I am all yours").

His accomplishments over nearly twenty-seven years as pope are far too lengthy to list here. I will note a few. He was a prolific writer, producing fourteen encyclicals, fourteen apostolic exhortations, eleven apostolic constitutions, forty-five apostolic letters, countless sermons, and other writings. He helped revise canon law and the universal catechism called for by Vatican II. He was widely traveled, bringing Christ's love to many regions of the world. He had a special love for the family and initiated the World Meeting of Families in 1984. As well, he loved young people and started World Youth Day, bringing millions of young people together from all over the world. This pontiff beatified and canonized more holy men and women than any pope before him. St. John Paul II understood Communism firsthand and recognized himself as the "bishop dressed in white" mentioned in the Third Secret of Fatima, who is killed by bullets and arrows shot at him by soldiers. This prodded the pope to carry out properly the Consecration that was asked by Our Lady.

It happened that on May 13, 1981 (the sixty-fourth anniversary of the first apparition in Fatima), John Paul II was seriously wounded in a burst of gunfire in St. Peter's Square from a would-be assassin. The pontiff suffered serious blood loss and was on the brink of death when he reached the hospital. When he regained consciousness, his very first thoughts were on Fatima. During his months of recuperation at the hospital, he began to read Sr. Lucia's memoirs and her letters. The pontiff then knew what he needed to read next. On July 18, St. John Paul II asked for the sealed envelope containing the Third Secret of Fatima.

He was very moved upon reading the contents of the envelope. The raw reality of the "secret" gave him a jolt. He immediately thought of consecrating the world to the Immaculate Heart of Mary. The Third Secret of Fatima was about him, the "bishop dressed in white." St. John Paul II believed that on May 13, 1981, the Blessed Mother guided the bullet to protect him from death. He recognized himself as the pope (or bishop) who, in the third part of the secret, was killed. As we know, St. John Paul II was not killed, but instead was miraculously saved by the Blessed Mother. He had no doubt about this. He said that the Blessed Mother saved him and gave him back his life.

St. John Paul II's former secretary, Cardinal Stanislaw Dziwisz, beautifully described the Blessed Mother's intervention to give back Pope John Paul II's life. He wrote:

Sunday

In Sr. Lucia's vision, he recognized his own destiny. He became convinced that his life had been saved—no, given back to him anew—thanks to our Lady's intervention and protection. It's true, of course, that the "bishop dressed in white" is killed in Sr. Lucia's vision, whereas John Paul II escaped an almost certain death. So? Couldn't that have been the real point of the vision? Couldn't it have been trying to tell us that the paths of history, of human existence, are not necessarily fixed in advance? And that there is a Providence, a "motherly hand," which can intervene and cause a shooter, who is certain of hitting his target, to miss? "One hand shot, and another guided the bullet" was how the Holy Father put it.[44]

St. John Paul II forgave his would-be assassin, Mehmet Ali Agca, and met with him. Agca asked him, "Why aren't you dead?" He couldn't understand why his bullets did not kill the pope. St. John Paul II believed wholeheartedly that the Blessed Mother guided the bullet that struck him. That bullet is now in the crown of the statue of Our Lady of Fatima in Portugal, at the request of St. John Paul II.

In the passage at the beginning of this chapter, St. John Paul II said that "redemption is always greater than man's sin and the 'sin of the world.' ... The heart of Mary is aware of this ... and so she calls us. She not only calls us to be converted: she calls us to accept her motherly help to return to the source of redemption."

Mother Mary calls to each one of us.

---

[44] Stanisław Dziwisz and Gian Franco Svidercoschi, *A Life with Karol: My Forty-Year Friendship with the Man Who Became Pope*, 1st American ed. (New York: Doubleday, 2008), 136.

WEEK 3: JOY

Reflect

Our Church is certainly rich because of the inspiration and wisdom given it through St. John Paul II. There is much to think about through today's reflection. We see that Fatima's messages are profound, mysterious, and quite simple. God loves us more than we can comprehend. He sends us Jesus' Mother, the beautiful Queen of Heaven, to intervene and to save us — to give our lives back. Through St. John Paul II's former secretary's words, we can be inspired to believe also "that there is a Providence, a 'motherly hand' which can intervene." Take time to ponder this.

Pray

Dear Jesus and Our Lady of Fatima, please help me to surrender my heart fully to God this Advent. Our Lady of Fatima and St. John Paul II, please pray for me.

Pray the Rosary today in honor of Our Lady of Fatima and for peace in the world.

Act

Offer a sacrifice in reparation for sinners, as Our Lady of Fatima has asked. Keep in mind that we live in a world of unbelievers. Strive to be an example of God's love to them. As well, work hard to convert your heart today with God's grace and Mother Mary's help, remembering that conversion of heart should be a daily occurrence.

ST. JOHN PAUL II EMPHASIZES MOTHERLY LOVE AND A CALL FROM THE GOSPEL

If the Church has accepted the message of Fatima, it is above all because that message contains a truth and a call whose basic content is the truth and the call of the Gospel itself. "Repent and believe in the gospel" (Mark 1:15): these are the first words that the Messiah addressed to humanity.... The Lady of the message seems to have read with special insight the "signs of the times," the signs of our time.

—St. John Paul II, Homily at Fatima, May 13, 1982

Read

On May 13, 1982, St. John Paul II visited Fatima. He said in his homily there, "And so I come here today because on this very day last year, in St. Peter's Square in Rome, the attempt on the Pope's life was made, in mysterious coincidence with the anniversary of the first apparition at Fatima, which occurred on May 13, 1917." He explained why he was there: "I seemed to recognize in the coincidence of the dates a special call to come to this place." The Holy Father wanted to give special thanks. He said, "And so, today I am here. I have come to thank Divine Providence in this place which the Mother of God seems to have chosen in a particular way. *Misericordiae Domini, quia non sumus consumpti* ('Through God's mercy, we were spared' [Lam. 3:22]), I repeat once more with the prophet."

St. John Paul II mentioned several things in his homily that day. He explained the Church's acceptance of the private revelation of the Fatima apparitions. "The Church has always taught and continues to proclaim that God's revelation was brought to completion in Jesus Christ, who is the fullness of that revelation, and that 'no new public revelation is to be expected before the glorious manifestation of our Lord' (*Dei Verbum*, 4). The Church judges private revelations by the criterion of conformity with that single public Revelation."

WEEK 3: JOY

During his homily, St. John Paul II spoke about the profound dimension of Mary's motherly love. He explained it this
way: "When Jesus on the Cross said: 'Woman, behold, your son'
(John 19:26), in a new way he opened his Mother's Heart, the
Immaculate Heart, and revealed to it the new dimensions and
extent of the love to which she was called in the Holy Spirit
by the power of the sacrifice of the Cross." Jesus gave us the
supreme gift of his own Mother. Mary's loving role is integral to
our salvation. She always leads us to her Son Jesus. "Do whatever he tells you," she told the servants at the wedding at Cana
(John 2:5) — words that are certainly meant for all of us.

The pontiff said, "In the words of Fatima we seem to find
this dimension of motherly love, whose range covers the whole
of man's path towards God, the path that leads through this
world and that goes, through Purgatory, beyond this world. The
solicitude of the Mother of the Savior is solicitude for the work
of salvation: the work of her Son." The Blessed Mother was
always completely tied to her Son's work of salvation. "It is solicitude for the salvation, the eternal salvation, of all," the pope
reminded us. He added, "Now that sixty-five years have passed
since that May 13, 1917, it is difficult to fail to notice how the
range of this salvific love of the Mother embraces, in a particular way, our century." Our Lady of Fatima's message spans the
decades and even centuries. Her message is clearly about conversion, about turning away from sin, about repentance, prayer, and
reparation. Because she is our Mother, she can't help but try to
save all her children.

In his homily, St. John Paul II continued, "In the light of a
mother's love we understand the whole message of the Lady of
Fatima. The greatest obstacle to man's journey towards God is
sin, perseverance in sin, and, finally, denial of God: the deliber-
ate blotting out of God from the world of human thought, the

detachment from him of the whole of man's earthly activity, and the rejection of God by man." These are sobering words but so true. We can't help but see this reality all around us and thus the great need to atone for this sin so that our brothers and sisters can make it to the heavenly banquet one day.

Reflect

St. John Paul II spoke often and lovingly of his Mother Mary and the profound dimension of her love. In our reflection today, we see St. John Paul II's sentiments on the message of Fatima and its call to the hearts of the faithful. The pontiff's words that begin our reflection today remind us to repent and believe in the gospel. During this holy season of Advent, let us consider what sins we need to repent of and what sacrifices we can make to atone for our sins and the sins of others.

Pray

Dear Jesus and Our Lady of Fatima, please help me to be more generous with others this Advent. Our Lady of Fatima and St. John Paul II, please pray for me.

Pray the Rosary today in honor of Our Lady of Fatima and for peace in the world.

Act

Offer a sacrifice in reparation for sinners, as Our Lady of Fatima has asked. Pray the Sacrifice Prayer often.

Each day, strive to convert your heart with God's grace and Mother Mary's help, remembering that conversion of heart should be a daily occurrence.

TUESDAY

THE PRAYER OF THE ROSARY HEALS TROUBLES IN THE CHURCH AND IN THE WORLD

The Rosary is my favorite prayer. A marvelous prayer. Marvelous in its simplicity and its depth.

— Pope St. John Paul II, *Rosarium Virginis Mariae*, no. 2

Read

The Rosary is not merely a string of beads with a crucifix attached. It is a centuries-old beloved prayer of the Catholic
Church and has an interesting background. Some say that the
use of beads to count prayers dates back to the Middle Ages. In
fact, the Desert Fathers used beads for keeping track of prayers in
the fourth century. The Rosary itself was gradually developed between the twelfth and fifteenth centuries. Tradition holds that St.
Dominic (d. 1221) received the Rosary from the Blessed Mother
and went on to preach the use of the Rosary through his mission-
ary work in France among the Albigensians, who did not believe
in the Incarnation of Christ. There is some disagreement about
whether the fully evolved Rosary was initiated by St. Dominic.
Some scholars say the Rosary is not mentioned in the earliest
accounts of his life, nor is he associated with the Rosary in any of
the Dominican constitutions. Some say that the Rosary took on
a long and gradual development beginning before St. Dominic's
time and that it had attained its final form well after St. Dominic's time. Whether or not St. Dominic devised the Rosary, he
certainly passionately and successfully preached its use to convert
sinners and those who had lost their faith. As well, several popes
have paid tribute to St. Dominic's affiliation with the Rosary. It
is believed that a miracle occurred when St. Dominic placed a

rosary over a possessed man's neck: thousands of demons were expelled. A couple of centuries later, Blessed Alain de La Roche (d. 1475) worked tirelessly to restore the devotion of the Rosary, which had fallen out of popularity. He established Rosary confraternities and developed the Dominican Rosary.

Some people complain that it takes too long to pray the Rosary or that it is repetitive. Venerable Archbishop Fulton Sheen artistically described the prayer of the Rosary. He said, "The Rosary is the book of the blind, where souls see and there enact the greatest drama of love the world has ever known; it is the book of the simple, which initiates them into mysteries and knowledge more satisfying than the education of other men; it is the book of the aged, whose eyes close upon the shadow of this world, and open on the substance of the next. The power of the Rosary is beyond description."[45]

Archbishop Sheen was certainly not the only one who believed in the power of the Rosary. Many of the saints and many popes have extolled its efficacy. St. John Paul II, in his Apostolic Letter *Rosarium Virginis Mariae*, teaches that although the Rosary has been around for ages, it "has lost none of the freshness." He said it is "destined to bring forth a harvest of holiness" (no. 1). St. Padre Pio called it the "weapon" for our time. He said, "Some people are so foolish that they think they can go through life without the help of the Blessed Mother. Love the Madonna and pray the Rosary, for her Rosary is the weapon against the evils of the world today. All graces given by God pass through the Blessed Mother."[46]

---

[45] Quoted in William Saunders, "History of the Rosary," EWTN, https://www.ewtn.com/library/answers/rosaryhs.htm.

[46] Quoted in Johnnette S. Benkovic, "The Rosary: Saint Padre Pio's Weapon against Evil," to Franciscan Spirit, June

Tuesday

The prayer of the Rosary is responsible for an amazing victory in the 1500s, when Muslim Turks attacked Eastern Europe. In 1571, Pope Pius V organized a fleet under the command of Don Juan of Austria, the half brother of King Philip II of Spain. The pope asked the faithful to pray that God would grant victory to the Christians through praying the Rosary and begging the Blessed Mother under the title of Our Lady of Victory. On October 7, 1571, the Christian and Muslim fleets fought the Battle of Lepanto. The Christian flagship flew a blue banner to symbolize Christ crucified. Although the Christians were ridiculously outnumbered, the Muslims were defeated in the battle. The following year, Pope St. Pius V established October 7 as the feast of the Holy Rosary. This beautiful feast reminds us of this great victory and calls us to be thankful and not to hesitate to beseech the Mother of God through her Rosary.

During his homily on May 13, 1982, St. John Paul II connected the Mother of God and her Rosary with the universal call to repentance. He stated, "The call to repentance is a motherly one, and at the same time it is strong and decisive. The love that 'rejoices in the truth' (cf. 1 Cor 13:6) is capable of being clear-cut and firm. The call to repentance is linked, as always, with a call to prayer." Our Lady of the Rosary requests our prayers and prays with us. Throughout her apparitions she asked the shepherd children to pray the Rosary daily. St. John Paul II pointed out, "In harmony with the tradition of many centuries, the Lady of the message indicates the Rosary, which can rightly be defined as 'Mary's prayer': the prayer in which she feels particularly united with us. She herself prays with us."

1, 2017, https://blog.franciscanmedia.org/franciscan-spirit/the-rosary-saint-padre-pios-weapon-against-evil.

WEEK 3: JOY

The Rosary is powerful. Sr. Lucia had poignantly stated, "The Most Holy Virgin in these last times in which we live has given a new efficacy to the recitation of the Rosary to such an extent that there is no problem, no matter how difficult it is, whether temporal or above all spiritual, in the personal life of each one of us, of our families, ... that cannot be solved by the Rosary. There is no problem, I tell you, that we cannot resolve by the prayer of the Holy Rosary."[47]

Reflect

As we move through this third week of Advent, we see that Lucia gives us great counsel about the Rosary's power to solve problems. St. John Paul II told us that Mother Mary prays with us when we pray the Rosary. We should find this to be quite amazing! The pontiff also reminded us of our responsibility to repent and that "the call to repentance is linked, as always, with a call to prayer." Our Lady of Fatima consistently requested the daily Rosary for peace, to prevent future catastrophes, and for the conversion of sinners. St. John Paul II told us that the Rosary is "destined to bring forth a harvest of holiness." Let's be sure to do our very best to pray the Rosary with attention and love, and let us pray that the triumph of Our Lady's Immaculate Heart be accomplished very soon.

Pray

Dear Jesus and Our Lady of Fatima, please help me not to be stingy in my prayers this Advent. Help me to be

---

[47] Conversation between Sr. Lucy of Fatima and Fr. Fuentes, December 26, 1957, quoted in Dominican Fathers of Avrille, "The Origin of the Rosary," Our Lady of the Rosary Library, https://olrl.org/sacramental/rosary.shtml.

Tuesday

generous like Lucia, Francisco, and little Jacinta! Our Lady of Fatima and St. John Paul II, please pray for me.

Pray the Rosary today in honor of Our Lady of Fatima and for peace in the world.

Act

Offer a sacrifice in reparation for sinners, as Our Lady of Fatima has asked. Offered lovingly, our sacrifices please God and help to convert sinners, as well as transform our own souls! Strive to convert your heart today with God's grace and Mother Mary's help, remembering that conversion of heart should be a daily occurrence.

WEDNESDAY

ST. JOHN PAUL II TELLS OF LITTLE FRANCISCO'S LOVE FOR JESUS

Francisco bore without complaints the great sufferings caused by the illness from which he died. It all seemed to him so little to console Jesus: he died with a smile on his lips.

> — St. John Paul II, Homily for the beatification of Francisco and Jacinta Marto (May 13, 2000)

Read

Young Francisco Marto was often very reserved because he was usually deep in thought or mightily praying to console God and to help convert sinners. He had a huge heart for a little boy and a spiritual maturity way beyond his years.

The Blessed Mother shed many graces upon him through her Immaculate Heart. She revealed great spiritual insights to Francisco about the importance of eternity and of saving souls. One time, little Francisco shared with his older cousin Lucia, "I loved seeing the Angel, but I loved still more seeing Our Lady. What I loved most of all was to see Our Lord in that light from Our Lady which penetrated our hearts. I love God so much! But He is so sad because of so many sins! We must never commit any sins again."[48]

The young shepherd was so passionate about consoling God and Mother Mary that he would often go off by himself and pray behind some rocks or a bush when he was out in the fields. He preferred to be in the church by the tabernacle with his "hidden Jesus," but he knew that he could pray anywhere. Lucia asked him one day why he went off by himself. He replied, "I prefer

---

[48] Apostoli, *Fatima for Today*, 18.

praying by myself so that I can think and console Our Lord, who is so sad!"[49]

Lucia later revealed that Francisco spoke very little, but that he usually did everything he saw his cousins doing. It was very rare for him to suggest anything himself. Lucia observed Francisco's heroic patience in his suffering throughout his debilitating illness, never complaining but always eager to offer it all up to God. Lucia shared in her memoirs, "While he was ill, Francisco always appeared joyful and content. I asked him sometimes, 'Are you suffering a lot, Francisco?' He immediately answered, 'Quite a lot, but never mind! I am suffering to console Our Lord, and afterwards, within a short time, I am going to heaven!'" Lucia desired his intervention in heaven, so she told her little cousin, "Once you get there, don't forget to ask Our Lady to take me there soon as well." But Francisco told her that he would not ask that because Our Lady had already told Lucia that she must stay a while longer.[50]

While preparing to die and go to his eternal reward, Francisco asked Lucia and Jacinta to remind him of any sins he might have committed during his life. He wanted to be sure he confessed everything to the priest before receiving Holy Communion. His death was very hard for both Lucia and Jacinta. However, his cousins clung tightly to Mother Mary's promises to them and the sure knowledge of the beautiful eternal life that awaited them. Lucia told in her memoirs about her emotional farewell to her brave and beloved little cousin. Lucia wrote, "That night I said goodbye to him. 'Goodbye, Francisco! If you go to heaven tonight, don't forget me when you get there, do you hear me?'" Francisco answered his older cousin,

[49] *Fatima in Lucia's Own Words*, 156.
[50] Ibid., 163.

"No, I won't forget. Be sure of that." Lucia continued, "Then, seizing my right hand, he held it tightly for a long time, looking at me with tears in his eyes." So, she asked him, "Do you want anything more?" Tears were running down her cheeks, too. He replied, "No!" in a low voice. He was quite choked up. Lucia recalled, "As the scene was becoming so moving, my aunt told me to leave the room." As Lucia left, she called out, "Goodbye then, Francisco! Till we meet in heaven, goodbye!"[51] Lucia also reported that the grief she suffered in losing Francisco was a thorn that pierced her heart for many years. Little Jacinta would be taken to heaven soon after, but while she awaited her turn, she also sorely grieved for her kind and loving brother.

St. John Paul II spoke glowingly about Francisco and Jacinta Marto at their beatification Mass. He pointed out their heroism in following Our Lady's requests and spoke about Francisco's loving heart and his desire to console Jesus. He said:

> What most impressed and entirely absorbed Bl. Francisco was God in that immense light which penetrated the inner depths of the three children. But God told only Francisco "how sad" he was, as he said. One night his father heard him sobbing and asked him why he was crying. His son answered: "I was thinking of Jesus who is sad because of the sins that are committed against him." He was motivated by one desire — so expressive of how children think — "to console Jesus and make him happy."[52]

[51] Ibid., 166.
[52] Pope John Paul II, Homily on the feast of Our Lady of Fatima and the Beatification of Jacinta and Francesco Marto (May 13, 2000), no. 2, http://www.ewtn.com/library/papaldoc/jjp2frja.htm.

The pontiff went on to speak of Francisco's radical spiritual transformation and his intense spiritual life, his mystical union with God, and his striving to atone for offenses against God, renouncing his own pleasures and not complaining about the great sufferings caused by the illness that eventually killed him. Little Francisco was an example of Christian heroism, offering many sacrifices for the conversion of sinners. This he accomplished through the various details of his daily life, and also through his fervent prayers before Jesus in the Blessed Sacrament—his "hidden Jesus"—where Francisco received Jesus' abiding love and peace.

St. John Paul II said, "Francisco bore without complaining the great sufferings caused by the illness from which he died. It all seemed to him so little to console Jesus: he died with a smile on his lips." He added, "Little Francisco had a great desire to atone for the offenses of sinners by striving to be good and by offering his sacrifices and prayers. The life of Jacinta, his younger sister by almost two years, was motivated by these same sentiments."[53]

Reflect

What can we learn from Francisco's love for Jesus and Mary and the souls of others, as well as from his heroic patience and perseverance in suffering? Can we, too, smile during suffering? With God's grace comes strength and courage. Take time today to ponder St. Francisco's life, and pray to be able to emulate his virtues.

[53] Ibid.

Wednesday

Pray

Dear Jesus and Our Lady of Fatima, please help me to be like St. Francisco this Advent. Our Lady of Fatima, St. John Paul II, and St. Francisco, please pray for me.

Pray the Rosary today in honor of Our Lady of Fatima and for peace in the world.

Act

Think of brave Francisco and offer lovingly a sacrifice in reparation for sinners, as Our Lady of Fatima has asked. St. John Paul II remarked about little Francisco, "It all seemed to him so little to console Jesus: he died with a smile on his lips." Can we be as generous? Strive to convert your heart today and every day with God's grace and Mother Mary's help, remembering that conversion of heart should be a daily occurrence.

THURSDAY

ST. JOHN PAUL II TELLS
OF LITTLE JACINTA'S
LOVE FOR OUR LADY

Little Jacinta felt and personally experienced Our Lady's anguish, offering herself heroically as a victim for sinners.

—St. John Paul II, Homily for the beatification of Francisco and Jacinta Marto (May 13, 2000)

Read

What can we say about Jacinta? Our Lady poured many graces upon her. Jacinta loved God with all her heart and deeply desired to help convert sinners. Lucia said in her memoirs that Jacinta possessed many endearing qualities and was a bright, vivacious child. Jacinta was certainly a very joyful little girl with a bounce in her step. She would often break into dancing out in the fields at the sound of some shepherd playing his flute. Many times, Francisco played his little flute, and both girls danced and twirled.

Jacinta was also very serious about fulfilling Our Lady's requests. Lucia said, "Ever since the day Our Lady taught us to offer our sacrifices to Jesus, any time we had something to suffer, or agreed to make a sacrifice, Jacinta asked: 'Did you already tell Jesus that it's for love of Him?' If I said I hadn't, she answered: 'Then I'll tell Him,' and joining her hands, she raised her eyes to heaven and said: 'O Jesus, it is for love of You, and for the conversion of sinners.' "[54] Lucia also said, "Jacinta's thirst for making sacrifices seemed insatiable."[55] After the apparitions of Our Lady of Fatima, Jacinta became much more serious because she

[54] *Fatima in Lucia's Own Words*, 50.
[55] Ibid., 47.

wanted to devote all her time to prayer. She even gave up dancing, which she absolutely loved. When Lucia asked her why she
gave up dancing, Jacinta simply and sincerely stated, "Because I
want to offer this sacrifice to Our Lord."[56]

Fr. Andrew had a special love for little Jacinta; he expressed
it to me many times! In his book *Fatima for Today*, he said,
"Like her brother, she loved nature because it made her think of
God. She also longed to receive Jesus in Holy Communion." Fr.
Andrew said that "she loved to hear about the Passion of Jesus
and meditate on it, which often moved her to tears. Her love
for God was so tender, she could not bear to hear anyone use his
name in vain." As well, Fr. Andrew said, "She did not want anyone ever to go to hell but wanted everyone to go to heaven."[57]

St. John Paul II expressed some endearing sentiments about
little Jacinta at her beatification Mass. He said:

Little Jacinta felt and personally experienced Our Lady's
anguish, offering herself heroically as a victim for sinners.
One day, when she and Francisco had already contracted
the illness that forced them to bed, the Virgin Mary came
to visit them at home, as the little one recounts: "Our
Lady came to see us and said that soon she would come
and take Francisco to heaven. And she asked me if I still
wanted to convert more sinners. I told her yes." And
when the time came for Francisco to leave, Jacinta said,
"Give my greetings to Our Lord and to Our Lady and tell
them that I am enduring everything they want for the
conversion of sinners." Jacinta had been so deeply moved
by the vision of hell during the apparition of July 13 that

[56] Ibid., 54.
[57] Apostoli, *Fatima for Today*, 18.

for her no mortification or penance seemed too great to save sinners.[58]

The pontiff further extolled Jacinta's great witness to the Faith and expressed his gratitude to her for her many prayers for him. He said:

She could well exclaim with St Paul: "I rejoice in my sufferings for your sake, and in my flesh I complete what is lacking in Christ's afflictions for the sake of his body, that is, the Church" (Col 1:24). Last Sunday at the Colosseum in Rome, we commemorated the many witnesses to the faith in the 20th century, recalling the tribulations they suffered through the significant testimonies they left us. An innumerable cloud of courageous witnesses to the faith have left us a precious heritage which must live on in the third millennium. Here in Fatima, where these times of tribulation were foretold, and Our Lady asked for prayer and penance to shorten them, I would like today to thank heaven for the powerful witness shown in all those lives. And once again I would like to celebrate the Lord's goodness to me when I was saved from death after being gravely wounded on May 13, 1981. I also express my gratitude to Bl. Jacinta for the sacrifices and prayers she offered for the Holy Father, whom she saw suffering greatly.[59]

Little Jacinta had tenderly and passionately said, "I so love the Immaculate Heart of Mary! It is the heart of our dear

---

[58] Ibid., 19.
[59] St. John Paul II, Homily for the beatification of Francisco and Jacinta Marto, (May 13, 2000), no. 4.

Mother in heaven! ... If I could only put into the hearts of all, the fire that is burning within my own heart, and that makes me love the Hearts of Jesus and Mary so very much!" Lucia attested after Jacinta's death that both adults and children were drawn to Jacinta and much admired her peaceful, holy demeanor.

Though she would die alone as the Blessed Mother had foretold, many came to visit her while she lay seriously ill in the hospital. Her presence was a consolation for others. Countless questions were fired away at the young child, which caused her more pain, but she shared with Lucia that she offered it all up for the conversion of sinners.

Lucia told of many miracles of grace unfolding in people's hearts as well as healings when Jacinta prayed to the Blessed Mother with and for the people who requested prayers from her. Lucia told in her memoirs about a man who testified that after he had prayed, Jacinta appeared to him when he was lost deep in the forest. The young visionary led him out to safety. Jacinta said upon questioning that she had no recollection of it at all. But she might have been given the gift of bilocation. Whatever the case, we know that she is a canonized saint in heaven and that we can ask for her powerful intercession.

Reflect

Little Jacinta was a girl on fire with love for Our Lord and Our Lady. If we could possess even a portion of her passion, we could make a huge difference in our world! Let us remember that little Jacinta heroically answered heaven's call in her mission to follow Our Lady of Fatima's requests that she become an example to the world. We too, must answer heaven's call in our own missions in life. Let us always pray for the graces we need. Take time to ponder St. Jacinta's attributes and virtues. Strive to emulate her love and heroism. Ask her to help you.

Thursday

Pray

Dear Jesus and Our Lady of Fatima, please help me to be like St. Jacinta this Advent. Our Lady of Fatima and St. John Paul II, please pray for me.

Pray the Rosary today in honor of Our Lady of Fatima and for peace in the world.

Act

As you have been pilgrimaging through Advent, hopefully you are thinking about lovingly offering works of mercy and sacrifices that can ultimately move mountains! Leave the mountains to God. He will work the miracles! Focus on the smaller stuff! That said, offer a sacrifice today, in reparation for sinners, as Our Lady of Fatima has asked. Strive to convert your heart today with God's grace and Mother Mary's help, remembering that conversion of heart should be a daily occurrence.

ST. JOHN PAUL II TELLS
OF LUCIA'S FIDELITY
TO HER MISSION

The visit of the Virgin Mary which Lucia, as a little girl, received at Fatima in 1917, together with her cousins Francisco and Jacinta, was the beginning of a unique mission to which she remained faithful to the end of her days.

—St. John Paul II, in a letter to Bishop Albino Mamede Cleto of Coimbra the day after Sr. Lucia died

Read

What can we say about Lucia, the oldest visionary at Fatima? Today, we will look at St. John Paul II's sentiments. But, first, I'll mention the gift of our free will and the holy joy that should be woven into it.

God has given us our own free will, but He desires that we follow his holy will. The *Catechism* teaches us that "God created man a rational being, conferring on him the dignity of a person who can initiate and control his own actions. God willed that man should be 'left in the hand of his own counsel,' so that he might of his own accord seek his Creator and freely attain his full and blessed perfection by cleaving to him."[60] Additionally, we learn, "The more one does what is good, the freer one becomes. There is no true freedom except in the service of what is good and just. The choice to disobey and do evil is an abuse of freedom and leads to 'the slavery of sin.'"[61] Will we always choose to do good? With love for God and a serious prayer life, we are well on our way.

---

[60] CCC 1730, quoting Pastoral Constitution on the Church in the Modern World *Gaudium et Spes* (December 7, 1965), 17; Sir. 15:14.
[61] CCC, no. 1733; cf. Rom. 6:17.

WEEK 3: JOY

We might ask this question, though: Is joy woven into the tapestry of our following the holy will of God? Joy should certainly be present—and even obvious to others who are observing. Many times, however, we fall short of embracing God's will. Not only that: we often run from it when it requires our sacrifice or effort. In addition, even when we accept God's will, we may do so with a bit of grumbling or complaining. This was not the case for any one of the three poor and basically uneducated visionaries. The children's faith drove them forward to embrace everything required of them. Faith is a beautiful virtue—a gift that is given to us at baptism and is meant to grow along with other virtues in our hearts. We must exercise this beautiful virtue so it grows even more. I'm reminded of Mother Teresa, who urged us to smile, especially when it was hard to do so, or when we encounter someone we don't really feel like smiling at! Do we smile at God?

After Francisco and Jacinta went to heaven, Lucia, as we know, was left behind to learn to read and write and, as it turned out, to become a nun in two congregations—starting off as a Dorothean and ending as a Carmelite. In particular, she was asked to carry the responsibility of Our Lady of Fatima's messages. This she did all the way to the grave at almost ninety-eight years of age. Amazingly, that "while longer" that the Blessed Mother had mentioned to Lucia very early on became a very long while! Yet Lucia grew in holiness through the details of each day and fully embraced her unique call—God's holy will for her.

The day following Sr. Lucia's death, St. John Paul II wrote a letter to Bishop Albino Mamede Cleto of Coimbra. In it he emphasized the joy with which Lucia embraced God's will in her life. He said:

> Sr. Lucia bequeaths to us an example of great fidelity to the Lord and joyous attachment to his divine will. I recall

with emotion my several meetings with her and the bonds of our spiritual friendship that grew stronger with time. I have always felt supported by the daily gift of her prayers, especially during the most difficult moments of trial and suffering. May the Lord reward her abundantly for her great and hidden service to the Church.

We can certainly learn much from Lucia, who remained faithful from childhood to stay the course joyfully and carry out God's will. This doesn't mean that things were easy or that she felt like smiling all the time. No. In fact, Lucia mentioned in her memoirs the many difficulties she faced in carrying out the mission entrusted to her and to her younger cousins, such as the numerous interrogations in which even priests tried to trip the children up. Though it was very difficult for the children, they rose to the occasion. Many times, they hid under beds, in fig trees, or in cornfields when they saw people approaching to question them! Lucia said, "It was priests especially who put us through the most rigorous cross-examinations, and then returned to question us all over again. Whenever we found ourselves in the presence of a priest, we prepared to offer to God one of our greatest sacrifices!"[62] Through it all, Lucia and her cousins trusted God and relied on continual help and grace from the Blessed Mother.

In continuing his letter to Bishop Cleto, St. John Paul II said, "I like to think that it was the Blessed Virgin, the same one whom Sr. Lucia saw at Fatima so many years ago, who welcomed her on her pious departure from earth to heaven." Further, he expressed his loving sentiments: "May the Blessed Virgin now accompany the soul of her devout daughter to the beatific encounter with the divine Bridegroom."

---

[62] *Fatima in Lucia's Own Words*, 106.

WEEK 3: JOY

Reflect

We might ask ourselves how we are using the gift of our free will. How are those beautiful theological virtues of faith, hope, and love, which were given to us at baptism, flourishing in our hearts and through our actions? Do we strive to embrace God's holy will for us, even during painful difficulties? Do we try to smile and accept God's holy will in our lives? We have much to ponder. As well, we can pray about and work on our attitudes. Are we joyful? We can ask Mother Mary for help!

Pray

Dear Jesus and Our Lady of Fatima, please help me take time to pray more and be more generous with my gifts this Advent. Sr. Lucia and St. John Paul II, please pray for me. Our Lady of Fatima, please pray for me.

Pray the Rosary today in honor of Our Lady of Fatima and for peace in the world.

Act

Be sure to offer a sacrifice in reparation for sinners, as Our Lady of Fatima has asked. Strive to convert your heart today with God's grace and Mother Mary's help, remembering that conversion of heart should be a daily occurrence.

ST. JOHN PAUL II AND MOTHER MARY ASSIST US ON OUR PILGRIMAGE

And so she calls us. She not only calls us to be converted: she calls us to accept her motherly help to return to the source of Redemption.

—St. John Paul II, Homily, May 13, 1982

Read

The third week of Advent is ending. Hopefully and prayerfully, you are growing in virtue. You are on a mini pilgrimage, after all. In today's reflection, St. John Paul II will teach us about the meaning of our pilgrimage through life. St. John Paul II spoke about how Our Lady of Fatima "calls us." He said she asks us to receive her motherly help. What does he mean? What if we are not particularly close to Mary? Let's look.

On May 13, 1982, St. John Paul II went on a pilgrimage to Fatima to observe and acknowledge the first anniversary of the attempt on his life and the sixty-fifth anniversary of Our Lady's first apparition at Fatima. He delivered a powerful homily there and spoke about Mother Mary's presence in our lives, God's mercy, spiritual motherhood, the need for conversion and repentance, the Rosary, the meaning of the Consecration, and God's love. He lamented the state of the world today, noting that many people have gone astray, but also that there is great hope. He said his heart rejoiced with hope at the Consecration he was carrying out.

In one part of his homily, he explained how Our Lord gave us His Mother and about Christ's heart being pierced:

On the Cross, Christ said: "Woman, behold, your son!" With these words he opened in a new way his Mother's heart. A little later, the Roman soldier's spear pierced the side of the Crucified One. That pierced heart became a sign of the redemption achieved through the death of the Lamb of God.[63]

On that special anniversary, the pontiff spoke of Mary's Immaculate Heart and how it is united spiritually with her Son's Heart:

The Immaculate Heart of Mary, opened with the words "Woman, behold, your son!" is spiritually united with the heart of her Son opened by the soldier's spear. Mary's heart was opened by the same love for man and for the world with which Christ loved man and the world, offering himself for them on the Cross, until the soldier's spear struck that blow.[64]

St. John Paul II explained the meaning of the consecration of the world to Mary's Immaculate Heart:

Consecrating the world to the Immaculate Heart of Mary means drawing near, through the Mother's intercession, to the very Fountain of life that sprang from Golgotha. This Fountain pours forth unceasingly redemption and grace. In it reparation is made continually for the sins of the world. It is a ceaseless source of new life and holiness.

Consecrating the world to the Immaculate Heart of the Mother means returning beneath the Cross of the Son. It means consecrating this world to the pierced Heart of the Savior, bringing it back "to the very source

---

[63] St. John Paul II, "Mary's Message of Love," homily (May 13, 1982), no. 8, http://www.ewtn.com/library/PAPALDOC/jp820513.htm.
[64] Ibid.

of its Redemption." Redemption is always greater than man's sin and the "sin of the world." The power of the Redemption is infinitely superior to the whole range of evil in man and the world.[65]

The pope assured us that Mary is acutely aware and that she calls us to conversion. But, not only that: she wants us to accept her motherly help.

The Heart of the Mother is aware of this, more than any other heart in the whole universe, visible and invisible.

And so she calls us. She not only calls us to be converted: she calls us to accept her motherly help to return to the source of Redemption.[66]

St. John Paul II pointed to his Consecration and our need to turn to Mary. It is not a one-time thing! He said:

Once more this act is being done. Mary's appeal is not for just once. Her appeal must be taken up by generation after generation, in accordance with the ever new "signs of the times." It must be unceasingly returned to. It must ever be taken up anew.

The pontiff spoke about the meaning of our pilgrimage through our lives finally to reach heaven one day. He explained how the people of God "is making its pilgrimage towards the eternal Jerusalem, towards 'the dwelling of God with men.'" At that time there will be no more pain or crying—every tear will be wiped away. "For the former things have passed away."[67]

[65] Ibid.
[66] Ibid.
[67] Ibid., no. 12.

He then encouraged us to see with the eyes of faith and emphasized how blessed we are with much grace during our pilgrimage and to have Mother Mary, who helps to save us. He stated:

> But at present the former things are still in existence. They it is that constitute the temporal setting of our pilgrimage.
>
> For that reason, we look towards him who sits upon the throne and says, "Behold, I make all things new" (Rev. 21:5).
>
> And together with the Evangelist and Apostle we try to see with the eyes of faith "the new heaven and the new earth"; for the first heaven and the first earth have passed away.
>
> But "the first heaven and the first earth" still exist about us and within us. We cannot ignore it. But this enables us to recognize what an immense grace was granted to us human beings when, during our pilgrimage, there shone forth on the horizon of the faith of our times this "great portent, a woman" (Rev. 12:1).
>
> Yes, truly we can repeat: "O daughter, you are blessed by the Most High God above all women on earth . . . walking in the straight path before our God . . . you have avenged our ruin."
>
> Truly indeed, you are blessed.
>
> Yes, here and throughout the Church, in the heart of every individual and in the world, may you be blessed, O Mary, our sweet Mother.[68]

[68] Ibid.

Saturday

Reflect

Take some time today to ponder God's great love for you and the gift of His Mother Mary to guide you on your pilgrimage through life. Take time to thank God for the gift of St. John Paul II and the Consecration he made. Pray to Our Lady of Fatima and ask her to grant you every grace you need to convert your heart and to be a radiant example of love and hope to others who are struggling on their pilgrimages.

Pray

Dear Jesus and Our Lady of Fatima, please help me to open my heart to God's graces this Advent. Help me also to be attentive — to stay awake — to open my heart to the stranger in my midst who needs my help. Our Lady of Fatima and St. John Paul II, please pray for me.

Pray the Rosary today in honor of Our Lady
of Fatima and for peace in the world.

Act

Offer a loving sacrifice in reparation for sinners, as Our Lady of Fatima has asked. Strive to convert your heart today and every day with God's grace and Mother Mary's help, remembering that conversion of heart should be a daily occurrence.

Week 4: Love

OUR LADY OF FATIMA AND MOTHER TERESA TEACH US AUTHENTIC, ABIDING LOVE

My daughter, look at My Heart surrounded with thorns with which ungrateful men pierce it at every moment by their blasphemies and ingratitude. You, at least, try to console me, and say that I promise to assist at the hour of death, with all the graces necessary for salvation, all those who, on the first Saturday of five consecutive months go to confession and receive Holy Communion, recite five decades of the Rosary and keep me company for a quarter of an hour while meditating on the mysteries of the Rosary, with the intention of making reparation to me.

—Our Lady of Fatima to Sr. Lucia

On this Fourth Sunday of Advent, we light our fourth Advent-wreath candle. It represents love! Strive to live your Faith fully alive with love during this week of Advent. This week we will look at Advent with Our Lady of Fatima at our side and through the eyes and heart of St. Teresa of Calcutta. St. Teresa of Calcutta, whom I often call Mother Teresa (since I knew her personally and she was such a beautiful mother to me) was connected to Our Lady of Fatima, as we shall see in the reflections this week.

MOTHER TERESA'S TENDER LOVE FOR MOTHER MARY

Mary, Mother of Jesus, be Mother to me now.

—St. Teresa of Calcutta, in a letter to the author

Read

Here we are beginning the final week of Advent! My dear friend Mother Teresa—St. Teresa of Calcutta—will usher us through this week. Mother Teresa had a tender spot in her heart for Mother Mary. She prayed countless Rosaries and relied on Mary for endless help, including arranging a cease-fire in Lebanon for Mother Teresa so that she could rescue abandoned handicapped children from a hospital. Mother Teresa was close to Mary and communicated with her often. At first, that special communing went both ways. Allow me to explain.

Before Mother Teresa founded her congregation, the Missionaries of Charity, she was a nun in the order of the Sisters of Our Lady of Loreto, a gifted teacher at St. Mary's School, and eventually, in 1944, principal of the school. In 1946, on the now famous date of September 10 (called "Inspiration Day" and celebrated yearly by the Missionaries of Charity), Mother Teresa traveled to Darjeeling, India, by train to make her yearly retreat. It was on that train ride that Mother Teresa received what she referred to as a "call within a call." Jesus spoke to her and asked her to take care of His poor. She was already a nun, but now she was being called to do something more—much more. As the train chugged along, and later, through a series of visions, Mother Teresa became acutely aware of Jesus' thirst for the salvation of souls. Jesus told her that He wanted "victims of love" who would "radiate his love to souls."[69] Mother Teresa wholeheartedly accepted Jesus' request and, over the next few months, received interior locutions and visions. The Lord beckoned to her, "Come, be my light."[70]

Earlier, I mentioned that Mother Teresa's communing with Mother Mary was initially a two-way conversation. In the beginning, Mother Teresa was aware of Mary's presence and love and could hear her voice. Then, shortly after Mother Teresa started the Missionaries of Charity, everything stopped—the locutions, the visions, and the mystical conversations. The small nun was left alone in her conviction to walk in faith as she carried out the work through love and trust. For Mother Teresa, this must have been like groping in the dark. It was the beginning of her very long Dark Night that we learned about after her death in 1997.

Not too long ago, I looked through my notebook filled with Mother Teresa's letters to me that she typed lovingly on an old typewriter in the night, after her other duties were finished. Some of the characters were typed askew, reminding me of the old age of the typewriter. That gave me reason to pause and consider the holy passion of the frail, faithful woman who sat before it to type away—striving to communicate with people the world over. I don't think I will ever fully understand why or even properly appreciate the fact that this living saint took the time for my family and me and for our needs. She was already busy with a myriad of demands that pulled at her attention, as well as the important needs of her congregation and the "poorest of the

[69] Donna-Marie Cooper O'Boyle, *Mother Teresa and Me: Ten Years of Friendship* (North Haven, CT: Circle Press, 2009), 33.
[70] Ibid., 34.

poor" whom she served all over the world. Still, every letter that Mother Teresa wrote to me pierced my heart with a tender and profound love that I cannot explain properly. In reading Mother Teresa's letters again, I found that some took on an entirely new meaning and implication as I read each word slowly and meditatively.

In October 1987, in one of her letters, my spiritual mother and marvelous mentor wrote to me, "Please continue praying and offering your sufferings for our Mother—she needs it most now." All these years later, I now understand more clearly what Mother Teresa was asking of me. At the time I received her letter, I didn't fathom its meaning. Mother Teresa's sandals being firmly planted on the ground, not up in some lofty spiritual cloud somewhere, this saintly nun was aware of the state of the world, as well as what Our Lady of Fatima had requested from three simple shepherd children and the world. The Blessed Mother asked for conversion of heart, the daily Rosary, and penance and sacrifice for poor sinners.

Mother Teresa, in turn, asked others to pray the Rosary and to offer their sufferings to our Mother in heaven. In just about every letter that Mother Teresa wrote to me (and there are twenty-two!), the petite saint asked me to pray to Our Lady and to pray the daily Rosary. She said to pray it "fervently" and to "cling to Our Lady. She will surely lead you to Jesus to know his will for you."

I am blessed to have been given so many holy reminders and much great wisdom from my dear Mother Teresa, and I wish to pass it along to you. I'll share a story about how that simple, powerful prayer in the passage beginning this chapter was taught to me by Mother Teresa.

It happened during a precarious pregnancy during which I had to be on complete bed rest for almost the full nine months.

I had a heart condition and a hemorrhaged uterus, and I had lost three babies earlier to miscarriage. I reached out to my dear Mother and asked her to please pray for me. Mother Teresa sent me a letter with a blessed Miraculous Medal, which I still wear. She told me to call on Mother Mary often and that Mary would help me. She also said I should pray, "Mary, Mother of Jesus, be Mother to me now." I prayed to Mary often and trusted God with my pregnancy. Thanks be to God, both my baby and I survived that pregnancy and my baby is now twenty-seven years old! I named her after the Blessed Mother and the Blessed Mother's mother—Mary-Catherine Anne.

Reflect

Some say that when we make plans, God laughs! Mother Teresa was comfortably established as a holy Loreto nun, teacher, and school principal. She didn't plan ever to leave her position. She later revealed that leaving the familiarity and comfort of the Loreto convent to establish the Missionaries of Charity congregation was harder than leaving her family when she first became a nun. Yet Mother Teresa walked forward in faith, prayed continually to the Blessed Mother for help, and inspired others to stay close to Mother Mary as well. As you enter this fourth week of Advent, take time to reflect on your prayer life and your faith or lack thereof. What changes can you make to trust God and allow Mother Mary more fully into your life?

Pray

Dear Jesus and Our Lady of Fatima, as Christmas is fast approaching, please help me wholeheartedly to trust God this holy season. St. Teresa of Calcutta, please pray for me. Our Lady of Fatima, please pray for me and be Mother to me.

Sunday

Pray the Rosary today in honor of Our Lady
of Fatima and for peace in the world.

Act

Offer a sacrifice (great or small) in reparation for sinners, as Our Lady of Fatima has asked. Strive to convert your heart today with God's grace and Mother Mary's help, remembering that conversion of heart should be a daily occurrence.

MOTHER TERESA SHOWS US THAT OUR LADY WATCHES OUT FOR US

Let us love each person with the same love that God loves each one of us—a tender and personal love.

—St. Teresa of Calcutta, website of
the Missionaries of Charity

Read

Today, we switch gears just a bit for a fascinating story about Mother Teresa. My friend Deacon Al Gambone shared a story about his responsibility in whisking Mother Teresa in and out of a Fatima Shrine. Growing up with vivid teachings of Our Lady of Fatima from his parents and the nuns who taught him, Al eventually secured a job at the Our Lady of Fatima Shrine in Washington, New Jersey.

In June 1985, Mother Teresa was scheduled to give a talk at the popular Fatima Shrine. Al told me, "After the shock of knowing that Mother Teresa was coming to the Shrine, we immediately began planning for her visit. One of my functions was to prepare for Mother Teresa's visit." He quickly added, "However, I can't take the credit for such a wonderful day." Al prayerfully prepared for the visit. "My prayer for months leading up to Mother's visit was to Our Blessed Mother. I asked Our Lady to do it all: 'Just guide me,' I prayed." Al organized many details that involved close communication with state and local police, the Sisters, the employees, and volunteers.

News reports stated that more than twenty thousand people came to see Mother Teresa that day at the Blue Army Shrine in Washington, New Jersey. Al said, "One report even said we had twenty-five thousand. It was a day that had me up before dawn in

my jeans and T-shirt, directing the crew on how to best get the
cars, buses, and people where they needed to go." Al then had
to change quickly into a suit and tie to get ready to meet Mother
Teresa, her Sisters, the bishop, and various dignitaries.

Al noted that "getting her into the Shrine was not an issue,
but getting her out was going to be." The staff had serious concerns. "In planning, we knew that we had to get Mother Teresa
in quietly and out quietly. The amount of people there would
be too great; because she was so small, there was a concern the
crowds might crush her."

When the Mass was over, Al and his coworkers jumped into
action to get Mother safely off the grounds. They had an un-
marked police car ready. "And we whisked her away with Mother
and me in the back of the car."

Reflecting on that day, Al recalled, "The one plan that I
didn't have was what to say to Mother once I was alone with
her." He reflected, "I knew that I was in the presence of a saint.
All I could think about was wondering if she could read my
soul. This was a scary thought." Even so, Al wanted to reassure
her. "I was very calm and told Mother what we were doing."
He recalled, "She had her rosary in her hands. She was wonderful to me, and I asked her if there was anything that I could
do for her." Mother Teresa answered, "Please, just take me to
my Sisters." Al said he would and handed the petite saintly
nun an envelope full of notes from people who wanted to reach
out to her. "I placed the envelope in her hands, and she put
it somewhere in her sari." He added, "I remember a feeling of
peace. Although I was nervous, Mother's presence had a calming effect on me, and I knew that I was safe as well."

One week later, Mother Teresa came back to the shrine
to thank all the employees and the Sisters who lived at the
Shrine for all they did. Al and his family were blessed to see the

humble, world-renowned, saintly nun again. Al said, "My father got a chance to meet her personally, and when he knelt down beside her, he cried as Mother held his hands."

Mother Teresa's visits were indeed memorable. The inspiring words expressed in her speech at the shrine were enjoyed by thousands of edified, faithful pilgrims. As well, all the behind-the-scenes details were keenly appreciated by Al Gambone and his family. Al's prayers for Our Lady of Fatima's guidance in his preparations were answered. "Our Lady was watching out for us," he concluded.

Reflect

Do you ask for Our Lady's guidance for big matters as well as in everyday details? As you are walking through these days of Advent, already now in the fourth week, be sure to prepare your heart for the fast-approaching Nativity of Our Lord Jesus as well as for His Second Coming. See if you can pause to look for a bit of prayerful silence today. Try to be more cognizant about limiting time spent on media and television to give yourself more prayer time. Try not to be distracted by the culture's shopping craziness. Try hard to carve out solid times for daily prayer and meditation. Make a sacrifice to offer in reparation for sinners.

Pray

Dear Jesus and Our Lady of Fatima, please help me to be lovingly attentive to those in my care each day this Advent. St. Teresa of Calcutta, please pray for me. Our Lady of Fatima, please pray for me.

Pray the Rosary today in honor of Our Lady
of Fatima and for peace in the world.

Act

Offer a sacrifice in reparation for sinners, as Our Lady of Fatima has asked. Hopefully, this has become a holy habit by now as you make your pilgrimage toward Christmas. Strive to convert your heart today with God's grace and Mother Mary's help, remembering that conversion of heart should be a daily occurrence.

MOTHER TERESA STANDS WITH MARY AT THE FOOT OF THE CROSS

With great love and trust stand with Our Lady near the Cross. What a gift of God!

—Mother Teresa, Instructions to novice mistresses, Casilina/Rome, June 30, 1997

Read

Mother Teresa was madly in love with Jesus and His holy
Mother. She chose the Immaculate Heart of Mary as her special
patroness and established that special feast day as the titular
feast for her congregation. We know that the Immaculate Heart
of Mary is a big part of Our Lady of Fatima's message. Mary's Immaculate Heart is full of love for all her children. But it is even
more than that.

I will share something rather contradictory. I just said that
Mary's heart was full, and it *is* full of love and grace, but someone else — a credible source — says it is empty. In his book
Mother Teresa: In the Shadow of Our Lady, Father Joseph Langford, MC, cofounder with Mother Teresa of her community of
priests, the Missionaries of Charity Fathers, writes, "The Immaculate Heart of Mary refers not only to Our Lady's love and
virtues, but also to her interior emptiness of self in imitation
of Christ who 'emptied himself' to save the human race." He
continues, "Our Lady's heart is the emptiest of all human hearts,
the emptiest of self and the emptiest of pride, and therefore the
most ready to give a heart's welcome and shelter to those who
are shelterless." Fr. Langford knows that Mother Teresa understood the mystery of Mary's Immaculate Heart: "Mother Teresa

saw this as the condition both for receiving and giving God to the full."[71]

Let's step back to those dusty, often unreliable train tracks, and that rickety steam train running slowly down them in 1946. It was nearing autumn, and the thirty-six-year-old Sister Teresa left Calcutta to head to West Bengal, where she departed in Siliguri to board the small train to Darjeeling on the last leg of her journey. As I mentioned earlier, she had received her "call within a call" on September 10, 1946, while sitting on that hot, crowded train en route to her annual retreat. As the train made its way on the tracks, amid the sometimes-deafening noise, the humble nun distinctively heard Jesus speaking to her heart. She became profoundly aware of her great and holy work ahead: taking care of the poor and the salvation of souls. After that very eventful train ride, Mother Teresa received countless extraordinary revelations from Jesus, informing her of the mission entrusted to her and reiterating what He wanted. This went on for over a year. Then, at the end of 1947, Jesus revealed a series of three visions to Mother Teresa. She was shown a crowd of the poor in each of the visions. In the first vision, she saw the reality and painful poverty of the poor, and their inner poverty. She saw herself in the scene and the poor were reaching out to her. In the second scene, the Blessed Mother was amid the poor with Mother Teresa kneeling at her side. Our Lady spoke to her:

Take care of them — they are mine. Bring them to Jesus — carry Jesus to them. Fear not. Teach them to say

---

[71] Joseph Langford, MC, *Mother Teresa: In the Shadow of Our Lady: Sharing Mother Teresa's Mystical Relationship with Mary* (Huntington, IN: Our Sunday Visitor, 2007), 42.

Tuesday

the Rosary, the family Rosary, and all will be well. Fear not—Jesus and I will be with you and your children.[72]

The Blessed Mother is intimately linked to God's call to Mother Teresa. In the third vision, the distressed crowd is in darkness, seemingly unaware of the presence of Jesus in their midst, hanging from the Cross. Our Lady and Mother Teresa are there, too. But, this time Mother Teresa saw herself as a little child. The Blessed Mother was supporting Mother Teresa, one hand on her shoulder and the other on Mother's outstretched arm. Our Lady was providing the strength that Mother Teresa needed in that moment. Mother Teresa's right arm was outstretched toward Jesus on the Cross. Jesus spoke to Mother Teresa.

"I have asked you. They have asked you. And she, my Mother, has asked you. Will you refuse to do this for me—to take care of them, to bring them to me?"[73]

With God's grace, and Mother Mary's incredible help, Mother Teresa was able courageously to give her fiat of acceptance for such an arduous and beautiful mission. Mother Mary was always nearby to support her as Mother Teresa carried out the work of striving to satiate the thirst of Jesus for the salvation of souls and to bring the poor to Jesus and Jesus to the poor. As well, the petite nun had the huge responsibility of managing her newly founded religious congregation and forming all her Sisters, and later, the brothers, priests, coworkers, and lay Missionaries of Charity who would follow. Again, Our Lady assisted Mother Teresa every step of the way.

[72] *Mother Teresa: Come Be My Light: The Private Writings of the "Saint of Calcutta,"* ed. Brian Kolodiejchuk, MC (New York: Doubleday, 2007), 99.
[73] Ibid.

WEEK 4: LOVE

Father Langford, who wrote about Mother Teresa and the Blessed Mother, spoke about the two in an interview. "As it was Our Lady who brought St. John, alone among the Twelve, to stand faithfully at Calvary," Fr. Langford explained, "so it was Our Lady who brought Mother Teresa through the sea of suffering opened before her, that she might shine the light of God's love on the poor."

Although the "two-way communication" that I mentioned earlier ceased when Mother Teresa endured the Dark Night, she continued to trust God and moved forward with love to accomplish God's holy mission entrusted to her. Mother Mary never left Mother Teresa's side.

Reflect

Has God redirected your life in some radical way? Do you think He can? Will you allow it? We cannot all be Mother Teresas, but we are all, without a doubt, called to a life of holiness. Mother Teresa often said that holiness is not a luxury of the few but a simple duty for all. Take time to ponder how Mother Teresa was devoted to Mother Mary and relied upon her for powerful help. As we read in the passage beginning today's reflection, Mother Teresa reminds us, "With great love and trust stand with Our Lady near the Cross."

Pray

Dear Jesus and Our Lady of Fatima, please help me to remember to turn to you often during this Advent, especially when I am suffering in some way. St. Teresa of Calcutta, please pray for me. Immaculate Heart of Mary, please pray for me. Help me to become a saint to bring glory to God!

Tuesday

Pray the Rosary today in honor of Our Lady
of Fatima and for peace in the world.

Act

Offer a sacrifice in reparation for sinners, as Our Lady of Fatima has asked. Can you consider a special (perhaps anonymous) Christmas gift you can give to someone in need? Continue to strive to convert your heart today with God's grace and Mother Mary's help, remembering that conversion of heart should be a daily occurrence.

MOTHER TERESA ENCOURAGES US TO BE LOVING LIKE MARY

Our prayer each day should be, "Let the joy of the Lord be my strength." Cheerfulness and joy were Our Lady's strength. This made her a willing handmaid of God. Only joy could have given her the strength to go in haste over the hills of Judea to her cousin Elizabeth, there to do the work of a handmaid. If we are to be true handmaids of the Lord, then we, too, each day, must go cheerfully in haste over the hills of difficulties.[74]

—Mother Teresa

[74] Mother Teresa, *Thirsting for God: Daily Meditations*, ed. Angelo Scolozzi (Cincinnati: Servant Books, 2013), 31–32.

Read

Certainly, Advent is a holy season of great joy. What better time to meditate on the Blessed Mother's virtues! Mother Teresa often referred to the Blessed Virgin Mary when speaking about the Faith and encouraged everyone to strive to emulate her virtues. For instance, Mother Teresa pointed out, "Cheerfulness and joy were Our Lady's strength." She encouraged us to imitate Mary in being a "willing handmaid" and cheerfully to set out to help those in need. As we know, this is what the young Mary did after giving her fiat to the Lord, declaring herself His handmaid, after the angel Gabriel had greeted her with the amazing message that she would become the Mother of God.

Even though she was entirely filled with the Holy Spirit, pregnant now with Jesus, and profoundly grateful to God, Mary didn't focus on her own situation or try to understand it fully, or even worry about what St. Joseph might think. Instead, she went "in haste" to help someone in need. That someone was the mother of St. John the Baptist, who was growing in Elizabeth's womb. Mary learned from the angel Gabriel that her cousin Elizabeth was in her sixth month of pregnancy in her old age and needed help. Mary was not afraid or hesitant to be a handmaid. She demonstrated a sacrificial love by putting aside her own pregnancy needs and heading out on an arduous trip to care for Elizabeth.

WEEK 4: LOVE

With Jesus growing in her immaculate womb, Mary hurried to Judea and entered the home of Elizabeth and Zechariah. St. John the Baptist leapt in Elizabeth's womb and the aging woman excitedly greeted her younger cousin. Mary then uttered her Magnificat song of praise:

> My soul magnifies the Lord,
> and my spirit rejoices in God my Savior,
> for he has regarded the low estate of his handmaiden.
> For behold, henceforth all generations will call me
> blessed;
> for he who is mighty has done great things for me,
> and holy is his name.
> And his mercy is on those who fear him
> from generation to generation.
> He has shown strength with his arm,
> he has scattered the proud in the imagination of their
> hearts,
> he has put down the mighty from their thrones,
> and exalted those of low degree;
> he has filled the hungry with good things,
> and the rich he has sent empty away.
> He has helped his servant Israel,
> in remembrance of his mercy,
> as he spoke to our fathers,
> to Abraham and to his posterity for ever.
>   (Luke 1:46–55)

One time, Mother Teresa explained how Mother Mary thanked God in her Magnificat and how she can help us:

The Magnificat is Our Lady's prayer of thanks. She can help us to love Jesus best; she is the one who can show us the shortest way to Jesus. Mary was the one whose inter-cession led Jesus to work the first miracle. "They have no wine," she said to Jesus. "Do whatever he tells you," she said to the servants. We take the part of the servants. Let us go to her with great love and trust.[75]

Mother Teresa pushes us forth to go with Mary—to go with great love and trust. In overseeing her congregation and in serving the poorest of the poor, Mother Teresa relied upon the Blessed Mother each day. She prayed heartily to Mary to help transform her heart and soul. We can pray Mother Teresa's prayer, too:

> Mary, I depend on you totally as a child on its mother, that in return you may possess me, protect me, and transform me into Jesus. May the light of your faith dis-pel the darkness of my mind; may your profound humil-ity take the place of my pride; may your contemplation replace the distractions of my wandering imagination; and may your virtues take the place of my sins. Lead me deeper into the mystery of the cross that you may share your experience of Jesus's thirst with me.[76]

Reflect

Do you have the heart of Mother Mary? How about the heart of Mother Teresa? Can your heart be joyful and more closely resemble theirs? Yes, it certainly can—with prayer! Are you willing to be a handmaid for the Lord—even you men? Mother Teresa reminds us, "If we are to be true handmaids of the Lord,

---

[75] Teresa and Angelo Devananda Scolozzi, *Total Surrender*, rev. ed. (Ann Arbor, MI: Servant Publications, 1985), 102.
[76] Mother Teresa, *Thirsting for God*, 17–18.

then we too, each day, must go cheerfully in haste over the hills of difficulties." Can we do that? As well, according to Mother Teresa, we take the part of the servants and should do whatever he tells us. Take time to ponder how Mother Mary fits into your life. Ask her to help you to be more generous and loving. For "extra credit," read Mary's Magnificat prayer above slowly and ponder the words, imagining her expressing it.

Pray

Our Lady of Fatima, with Christmas fast approaching, please lead me closer to your Son Jesus this holy season. Jesus, help me to be a joyful reflection of your Mother. Our Lady of Fatima and St. Teresa of Calcutta, please pray for me.

Pray the Rosary today in honor of Our Lady of Fatima and for peace in the world.

Act

Offer a sacrifice in reparation for sinners, as Our Lady of Fatima has asked. Who, especially, could use some love and cheer at this time of year? Reach out in love. Strive to convert your heart today with God's grace and Mother Mary's help, remembering that conversion of heart should be a daily occurrence.

THURSDAY

MOTHER TERESA'S HEARTFELT PRAYERS FOR THE CONSECRATION OF RUSSIA

I am not only the Queen of Heaven, but also the Mother of Mercy.

—Our Lady of Fatima

Read

When Mother Teresa was a Loreto Sister, having a tender devotion to the Mother of God, she created a little shrine to Our Lady of Fatima. Later, as the founder of the Missionaries of Charity, Mother Teresa established the Immaculate Heart of Mary as the patroness of the congregation. As we know, Mary's Immaculate Heart is an integral part of Our Lady of Fatima's messages. All throughout her ministry, Mother Teresa promoted the message of Fatima to the poor and the needy whom she served.

I discovered something incredible about Mother Teresa, her amazing connection with the message of Our Lady of Fatima, and her deep desire to pray for the conversion of Russia. Not only that: I also learned of a secret mission the petite nun devised that involved the Kremlin! I learned the story as I was doing research for my earlier two Fatima books.

I'll start with the fact that Mother Teresa gave out countless Miraculous Medals. I was the happy recipient of several of them, and as I mentioned, I still wear the one that she gave me during a precarious pregnancy. The front and back of the Miraculous Medal depict catechetical lessons about Jesus Christ, the Church, the Redemption, the Eucharist, grace, divine mercy, Original Sin, and the Blessed Mother as the Immaculate

Conception, crushing the head of the serpent. As well, we see symbols representing death, judgment, heaven, and hell. Amazingly—it's all there. In addition, the covenant of the two Hearts, the Sacred Heart of Jesus encircled with thorns and the Immaculate Heart of Mary pierced by a sword, are on the back of the medal. Mother Teresa was intensely drawn to these two Hearts.

Mother Teresa knew the power in Mary's magnificent graces with which she imbues the faithful through her amazing medal; therefore, Mother Teresa gave this medal to those she met—far and wide. She also placed them in properties she felt needed blessing or protection. She placed one in a property where she wanted to have a convent. Shortly after, the papers were signed, and the Sisters moved in!

Because Mother Teresa was devoted to Our Lady of Fatima, she was aware of the necessity of the Consecration of Russia, which Mary had requested. As well, Mother Teresa, being born in Skopje, in Kosovo, was of Slavic blood. Because of this, she felt close to the Russian people. It pained her deeply that Soviet Communism horrendously persecuted all forms of religion. Mother Teresa decided to smuggle a blessed Miraculous Medal into the Kremlin on the day that Pope John Paul II consecrated the world to the Immaculate Heart of Mary! This was a woman of faith—and action, I might add!

Through much prayer, perseverance, and a couple of courageous helpers, Mother Teresa accomplished her goal in getting the medal into the Kremlin on March 25, 1984, at the time of St. John Paul II's consecration. In addition, over the years, Mother Teresa was able to smuggle countless blessed Miraculous Medals into Russia with the help of holy friends.

Later, in 1988, Mother Teresa was invited to Moscow for an international meeting. She met Raisa Gorbachev, the wife of the secretary-general of the Soviet Union. The two women became friends, and Mother Teresa felt inspired to confide to Mrs. Gorbachev her wish to open convents in Russia. Mrs. Gorbachev promised to help. The first convent opened just one year later. Mother Teresa had hoped to open fifteen convents and was blessed that, over time, twenty were established!

Reflect

Take time to ponder Mother Mary in your life. At the start of this chapter, we read her words, "I am not only the Queen of Heaven, but also the Mother of Mercy." The Queen of Heaven loves her children intensely and wants us to know that she is also the Mother of Mercy. Can we turn to her with all our needs? Can we plead mercy from her for our family members, for our neighbors, for our communities, and for sinners?

Pray

Dear Jesus and Our Lady of Fatima, this Advent, please help me to do my part in spreading the Faith as Mother Teresa did. St. Teresa of Calcutta, please pray for me to be more courageous in sharing my Faith. Our Lady of Fatima, please pray for me.

Pray the Rosary today in honor of Our Lady of Fatima and for peace in the world.

Act

Offer a sacrifice in reparation for sinners, as Our Lady of Fatima has asked. Strive to convert your heart today with God's grace and Mother Mary's help, remembering that conversion of heart should be a daily occurrence.

MOTHER TERESA PUTS LOVE, FAITH, AND MERCY INTO PRACTICE

Mother Teresa, in all aspects of her life, was a generous dispenser of divine mercy.

—Pope Francis, homily at St. Teresa's
canonization, September 4, 2016

Read

We are moving swiftly toward Christmas! There's much to do, no doubt, but take a breath and sink yourself into the remaining reflections, striving for additional times of prayer in which to listen to Jesus speak to your heart. Allow St. Teresa of Calcutta to walk you through these final reflections.

Love and mercy go hand in hand. This week of Advent has been all about love. To be loving Christians, we must be merciful toward others. We need to recognize that we cannot get along in the spiritual life with only our faith. As Scripture teaches, even the demons believe. Do we want to be like them? I certainly don't think so! Remember the words of Scripture:

> What does it profit, my brethren, if a man says he has faith but has not works? Can his faith save him? If a brother or sister is ill-clad and in lack of daily food, and one of you says to them, "Go in peace, be warmed and filled," without giving them the things needed for the body, what does it profit? So faith by itself, if it has no works, is dead.
>
> But some one will say, "You have faith and I have works." Show me your faith apart from your works, and I by my works will show you my faith. You believe that

WEEK 4: LOVE

God is one; you do well. Even the demons believe—and shudder. (James 2:14–19)

Without a doubt, as a loving woman of great faith, Mother Teresa outwardly displayed that faith through her beautiful works. In addition, she put her beautiful virtues of love and faith into action to go forth and show God's mercy to count-less others, especially the poor, the "least" and most vulnerable among us. It was God's great mercy operating through Mother Teresa. So, we can say that the theological virtues of faith, hope, and love were on fire in this nun's heart and soul, and the flames of God's ardent love through Mother Teresa spread like wildfire to all she met and to all she served. As someone blessed to have been near this humble saint on many occasions, I can attest to that burning love that radiated from her very tiny being!

Pope Francis, at Mother Teresa's canonization, spoke about her merciful heart and the fact that she was "salt" and "light" to a darkened world. He said:

> Mother Teresa, in all aspects of her life, was a generous dispenser of divine mercy, making herself available for everyone through her welcome and defense of human life, those unborn and those abandoned and discarded. She was committed to defending life, ceaselessly proclaiming that "the unborn are the weakest, the smallest, the most vulnerable." She bowed down before those who were spent, left to die on the side of the road, seeing in them their God-given dignity; she made her voice heard before the powers of this world, so that they might recognize their guilt for the crime—the crimes!—of poverty they created. For Mother Teresa, mercy was the "salt" which gave flavor to her work; it was the "light" which shone in

the darkness of the many who no longer had tears to shed for their poverty and suffering.[77]

Although Mother Teresa became known all around the globe, she always tried to keep a low profile, to remain small and humble—just doing the work that God called her to do, not creating any fanfare or drawing attention to herself. She didn't want publicity. Yet, when you do the kind of powerful work that Mother Teresa did, people start noticing and the world starts changing for the better! If only we could all open our hearts to God's holy will in our lives so that we could bring His love to the "least" among us.

Mother Teresa taught others how to spread God's love in simple ways. One such way that I mentioned earlier in our Advent pilgrimage was by a simple smile. A smile can transform someone's heart. Smiling is something we can all do—and it's free! There should be no reason why we can't share smiles as often as possible. Experts say that smiling even helps us to be happier! A warm, loving smile is an act of mercy! Pope Francis mentioned Mother Teresa's famous smile in his homily at her canonization. He encouraged the faithful and said:

> May this tireless worker of mercy help us increasingly to understand that our only criterion for action is gratuitous love, free from every ideology and all obligations, offered freely to everyone without distinction of language, culture, race or religion. Mother Teresa loved to say, "Perhaps I don't speak their language, but I can smile." Let us carry her smile in our hearts and give it to those whom we meet along our journey, especially those who suffer. In

[77] Pope Francis, homily at St. Teresa's canonization (September 4, 2016).

WEEK 4: LOVE

this way, we will open opportunities of joy and hope for
our many brothers and sisters who are discouraged and
who stand in need of understanding and tenderness.[78]

Reflect

What can we learn about love and mercy in Our Lady of Fatima's message? Take time to ponder some of our earlier reflections
on Our Lady's message. Pope Francis proclaimed at Mother
Teresa's canonization, "Mother Teresa, in all aspects of her life,
was a generous dispenser of divine mercy." Our Lord and Our
Lady of Fatima call all of us to be generous dispensers of divine
mercy. Ponder ways in which you can do a better job of dispens-
ing mercy this Advent and beyond. Pray and ask for help.

Pray

Dear Jesus and Our Lady of Fatima, please help me to be
a much better dispenser of divine mercy this Advent and
Christmas. Our Lady of Fatima and St. Teresa of Calcutta,
please pray for me.

*Pray the Rosary today in honor of Our Lady
of Fatima and for peace in the world.*

Act

As often as you can, offer a loving sacrifice in reparation for
sinners, as Our Lady of Fatima has asked. Strive to convert your
heart today with God's grace and Mother Mary's help, remembering that conversion of heart should be a daily occurrence.

[78] Ibid.

MOTHER TERESA ENCOURAGES US TO STAY CLOSE TO OUR LADY

Stay very close to Our Lady. If you do this, you can do great things for God and for the good of people.[79]

—Mother Teresa

[79] Langford, *Mother Teresa*, back cover.

Read

Right from the very beginning, Mother Teresa taught her Sisters always to turn to Our Lady in every need and to rely upon her for spiritual and concrete help. Mother Teresa told them that they should cling to Our Lady like little children. Mother Teresa certainly clung to Mary, who was a constant companion and a continual support to this saint of the gutters, even (and perhaps especially) when Mother Teresa could no longer feel Mary's presence or hear the whispers to her heart and soul. Mother Teresa was united with the Mother of God in spirit at the foot of the Cross to hear Jesus' thirst for love — His thirst for the salvation of souls.

Mother Teresa, who had entrusted her work to the Blessed Mother's Immaculate Heart, asked the Blessed Virgin to take care of her congregation. She prayed:

> Immaculate Heart of Mary, cause of our joy, bless your own Missionaries of Charity. Help us to do all the good we can. Keep us in your most pure Heart, so that we may please Jesus through you, in you, and with you.[80]

[80] Ibid., 72.

WEEK 4: LOVE

This tireless saint of the gutters knew well Our Lady of
Fatima's requests to pray the Rosary daily for peace in the world.
She wholeheartedly recognized that the Rosary was not simply a
bunch of repetitious prayers. Whether on her fingertips or with
rosary beads in hand, Mother Teresa prayed countless fervent
Rosaries for God's holy will to be accomplished through her
society, founded in response to Jesus' requests to her.

Years ago, I was invited to a private event at which Cardinal John O'Connor would be honored. I'll mention here that
Cardinal O'Connor loved Mother Teresa and heartily welcomed
her and her Sisters in New York, where she opened convents
in the Bronx, in Brooklyn, and in Harlem. On the way to New
York City, I was inspired to stop at a little religious-goods store,
St. Joseph's Corner, to get a rosary to give to the cardinal. Later,
when the opportunity presented itself at the gathering, I handed
the rosary to my one-year-old son Joseph, who was sitting on my
lap, and Joseph handed it to the cardinal. He looked surprised
and asked why we were giving him the rosary. I explained that I
had been inspired to stop and get a rosary for him, and he smiled
and said something I find rather fascinating. "It's just so interesting and providential that you should give me these," he said. "I
just gave my Rosary beads to Mother Teresa yesterday because
she had just given hers away."

It was a wonderful blessing to be somehow mystically linked
in that exchange of rosaries with two people whom I considered
to be living saints. Our Lord never ceases to amaze me. I suppose
I shouldn't be surprised—He is God, after all!

In concluding our week on Mother Teresa and Our Lady of
Fatima, I will quote from *The Love That Made Mother Teresa*, by
David Scott, who elaborates on Mother Teresa's connection with
Our Lady of Fatima and her request for the consecration of Russia
to the Immaculate Heart of Mary. He writes: "On the day Mother

Teresa died, her sisters laid her in state beneath Our Lady of Fatima, a statue of the Blessed Mother depicted as she appeared to the children at Fatima. It was fitting in a way that no one could have known at the time."[81] Scott shines a light on Mother Teresa's close work with the Blessed Mother and "the revolution of love that God was working" through the tiny saint. He writes:

Few knew that she had been guided all these years by apparitions and a voice heard one summer long ago. And few knew that she was in the world to show Mary's love for her children, to show us the blessed fruit of Mary's womb, Jesus. We can now see that Mother Teresa was among the first fruits of the pope's consecration of the world to Mary's Immaculate Heart. The child called Gonxha — "flower bud" — became the first bud of new Christian life, flowering from the century's bloody soil of wars, famines, and persecutions.

Mother Teresa had followed the call of the gospel and done all that had been asked of her by Jesus and Mary in those 1946 visions. They were visions for which her whole life had prepared her — and visions that she lived out for all generations to come. Kept secret during her lifetime, these things have been disclosed to us now in the early days of the new millennium so that we might understand more fully the meaning of Mother Teresa and the revolution of love that God was working in our midst.[82]

---

[81] David Scott, *The Love That Made Mother Teresa: How Her Secret Visions and Dark Nights Can Help You Conquer the Slums of Your Heart* (Manchester, NH: Sophia Institute Press, 2016), 107–113.
[82] Ibid.

WEEK 4: LOVE

Reflect

Christmas is coming soon! Mother Teresa encourages us to "stay very close to Our Lady." She wholeheartedly knew that the Blessed Mother will lead us ever closer to her Son Jesus. How can you get closer to Mary? Certainly, you can in your prayers. But could you also talk to Mary more often? Remember, Mother Teresa encouraged her Sisters and me to call on Mother Mary often. She taught me that simple powerful prayer: "Mary, Mother of Jesus, be Mother to me now." Strive to call on Mary often. She will be sure to say lovingly to you, "Do whatever He tells you."

Pray

Dear Jesus and Our Lady of Fatima, please help me to be a shining witness of God's love this Christmas season. Our Lady of Fatima and St. Teresa of Calcutta, please pray for me.

Pray the Rosary today in honor of Our Lady of Fatima and for peace in the world.

Mother Teresa prayed often to the Immaculate Heart of Mary. We, too, can pray her prayer:

O most pure heart of Mary, allow me to enter your heart, to share your interior life. You see and know my needs; help me to do "whatever Jesus tells me" ... that my human needs may be changed into thirst for God alone. I desire to discover, satiate, and proclaim Jesus's thirst, but I know all too well my weakness, nothingness, and sin. Mother, may this covenant of consecration with you be the hidden strength in my life that you may use me to

satiate your Son to the full. Let this be my only joy ...
and you will be the cause of that joy.[83]

Act

Offer a sacrifice in reparation for sinners, as Our Lady of Fatima
has asked. Strive to convert your heart today and every day with
God's grace and Mother Mary's help, remembering that conversion of heart should be a daily occurrence. Try your best to keep
the prayerful meditative spirit that you have developed throughout your Advent pilgrimage. Continue to strive to learn more
about your Faith and to really and truly live it! God bless you!
Merry Christmas!

---

[83] Mother Teresa, *Thirsting for God*, 18.

ACKNOWLEDGMENTS

I am deeply grateful to my parents, Eugene Joseph and Alexandra Mary Cooper, for bringing me into the world and raising me in a large Catholic family. To my brothers and sisters—Alice Jean, Gene, Gary, Barbara, Tim, Michael, and David—thank you for being a wonderful part of my life.

My heartfelt gratitude goes to my husband, Dave, and my beloved children—Justin, Chaldea, Jessica, Joseph, and Mary-Catherine—for their continued love and support, and to my precious grandsons, Shepherd and Leo. I love you all dearly!

The wisdom and teachings of the Catholic Church have sustained me in my faith, along with the wonderful saints of the Church (too many to mention), guiding me through the twists and turns of life. Most especially, I am deeply grateful to Jesus, Mary, and Joseph, St. Mother Teresa, Servant of God Fr. John Hardon, SJ, Venerable Fulton Sheen, St. John Paul II, St. Francisco, St. Jacinta, Sr. Lucia, St. Faustina, St. Padre Pio, St. Catherine Labouré, St. Bernadette, St. Thérèse, St. Rita, and so many more of God's faithful children have illuminated my path. Any blessings I have received, I wish to pass along to you, my dear reader.

ADVENT WITH OUR LADY OF FATIMA

I owe a very special thanks to Sophia Institute Press for asking that I write this book—especially to Charlie McKinney, to John Barger for his very helpful suggestions, and to the wonderful team at Sophia Institute Press who helped get this book out to you!

Finally, I am extremely thankful to my readership, viewership, and listenership and to all those I meet in my travels. I pray for you every day. Thank you for being part of my fascinating pilgrimage through life! Please pray for me. I pray that God will continue to bless you in great abundance! May Our Lady of Fatima pray for us all!

ABOUT THE AUTHOR

Donna-Marie Cooper O'Boyle never planned to be an author,
TV host, or international speaker. Then again, she always desired to help others by sharing the Faith. It was during a precarious pregnancy, when God put her on complete bed rest, that
Donna-Marie was deeply inspired to begin writing books.

Because of God's amazing grace, Donna-Marie is a Catholic
wife, a mother of five children, a grandmother, and an award-
winning and best-selling author and journalist, TV host, international speaker, and pilgrimage and retreat leader. She is the
EWTN television host of *Everyday Blessings for Catholic Moms*,
Catholic Mom's Cafe, and *Feeding Your Family's Soul*, which she
created to teach, encourage, and inspire Catholic families. Her
love for children and imparting the Faith spurred her on to
serve as a catechist for almost thirty years. She is an extraordinary minister of the Eucharist in her parish. Donna-Marie
was noted as one of the Top Ten Most Fascinating Catholics in
2009 by *Faith & Family Live*. She enjoyed a decade-long friendship with Mother Teresa of Calcutta, became a Lay Mission-
ary of Charity, and started a branch of the Lay Missionaries of
Charity. For many years, her spiritual director was Servant of

God John A. Hardon, SJ, who also served as one of Mother Teresa's spiritual directors.

In 2008, Donna-Marie was invited by the Holy See to participate in an international congress for women at the Vatican to mark the twentieth anniversary of the apostolic letter *Mulieris Dignitatem* (*On the Dignity and Vocation of Women*). She received apostolic blessings from St. John Paul II and Pope Benedict XVI for her books and work and a special blessing from St. John Paul II for her work with St. Teresa of Calcutta. Donna-Marie has received awards from the Catholic Press Association, the Connecticut Press Club, and the National Federation of Press Women for her books, and a Media Award from the American Cancer Society for her volunteer column on cancer victims and survivors.

Donna-Marie is the author of more than twenty-five books on faith and family, including her memoir *The Kiss of Jesus: How Mother Teresa and the Saints Helped Me to Discover the Beauty of the Cross*. Donna-Marie's work has been featured in several Catholic magazines, in national newspapers, and on several websites and Internet columns. Some of her articles have been featured in *L'Osservatore Romano*, *Magnificat* magazine, the *National Catholic Register*, *Catholic World Report*, *Our Sunday Visitor*, and more. In addition to her own television shows, Donna-Marie has been profiled on many other television shows, including *Fox News*, *Rome Reports*, *Vatican Insider*, and on *EWTN News Nightly*, *Women of Grace*, *Sunday Night Prime*, *EWTN Live*, *At Home with Jim and Joy*, *The Journey Home*, and *Faith & Culture*. She is a regular guest on national and international radio shows as well and has hosted her own show.

Most of all, Donna-Marie strives to live in the present moments of life, where she discovers many beautiful opportunities to reach out with Christ's love to others. She encourages others

About the Author

to do the same. Donna-Marie lives with her family in beautiful rural New England, admiring God's creation. She lectures throughout the world on topics relating to Catholic and Christian women, faith, family, the saints, and her friend Mother Teresa. She can be reached at her websites, www.donnacooperoboyle.com and www.feedingyourfamilyssoul.com, where you can learn more about her books, ministry, and pilgrimages, and where she also maintains blogs.

Sophia Institute

Sophia Institute is a nonprofit institution that seeks to nurture the spiritual, moral, and cultural life of souls and to spread the Gospel of Christ in conformity with the authentic teachings of the Roman Catholic Church.

Sophia Institute Press fulfills this mission by offering translations, reprints, and new publications that afford readers a rich source of the enduring wisdom of mankind.

Sophia Institute also operates two popular online Catholic resources: CrisisMagazine.com and CatholicExchange.com.

Crisis Magazine provides insightful cultural analysis that arms readers with the arguments necessary for navigating the ideological and theological minefields of the day. *Catholic Exchange* provides world news from a Catholic perspective as well as daily devotionals and articles that will help you to grow in holiness and live a life consistent with the teachings of the Church.

In 2013, Sophia Institute launched Sophia Institute for Teachers to renew and rebuild Catholic culture through service to Catholic education. With the goal of nurturing the spiritual, moral, and cultural life of souls, and an abiding respect for the role and work of teachers, we strive to provide materials and programs that are at once enlightening to the mind and ennobling to the heart; faithful and complete, as well as useful and practical.

Sophia Institute gratefully recognizes the Solidarity Association for preserving and encouraging the growth of our apostolate over the course of many years. Without their generous and timely support, this book would not be in your hands.

www.SophiaInstitute.com
www.CatholicExchange.com
www.CrisisMagazine.com
www.SophiaInstituteforTeachers.org

Sophia Institute Press® is a registered trademark of Sophia Institute.
Sophia Institute is a tax-exempt institution as defined by the
Internal Revenue Code, Section 501(c)(3). Tax I.D. 22-2548708.